Folk Tales from the North York Moors

Peter Walker is the author of a number of highly successful thrillers. As Nicholas Rhea, he has written *Portrait of the North York Moors* and the popular 'Constable' series. As Peter Walker he has written *Murders and Mysteries From the North York Moors*.

He recently retired as an Inspector with the North Yorkshire Police to concentrate on his writing. He is married with four adult children and lives in Ampleforth.

FOLK TALES FROM THE NORTH YORK MOORS

Peter N. Walker

ROBERT HALE · LONDON

© *Peter N. Walker 1990*
First published in Great Britain 1990

Robert Hale Limited
Clerkenwell House
Clerkenwell Green
London EC1R 0HT

British Library Cataloguing in Publication Data

Walker, Peter N. (Peter Norman), *1936–*
Folk tales from the North York Moors.
1. North York Moors tales & legends – Anthologies
I. Title
398.2'09428'46

ISBN 0-7090-3975-1

Photoset in North Wales by
Derek Doyle & Associates, Mold, Clwyd.
Printed in Great Britain by
St Edmundsbury Press Ltd, Bury St Edmunds, Suffolk.
Bound by Hunter & Foulis Limited.

Contents

6   *Folk Tales from the North York Moors*

Folk Tales from the North York Moors

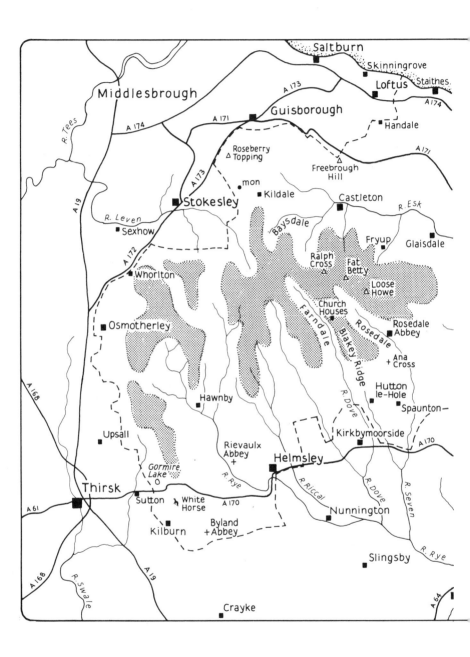

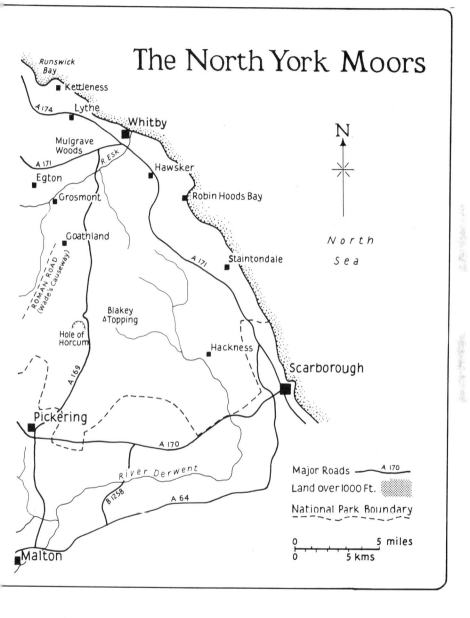

The North York Moors

Runswick Bay

Kettleness

A 174

Lythe

Whitby

Mulgrave Woods

R. Esk

A 171

Hawsker

Egton

Grosmont

Robin Hoods Bay

Goathland

ROMAN ROAD (Wade's Causeway)

A 171

Staintondale

Blakey △Topping

North Sea

Hole of Horcum

A 169

Hackness

Scarborough

Pickering

A 170

River Derwent

B 1258

A 64

Malton

N

Major Roads ——— A 170
Land over 1000 Ft.
National Park Boundary

0   5 miles
0   5 kms

Author's Preface

In selecting stories for this volume, I have endeavoured to include some lesser-known yarns but have avoided those which are purely accounts of ghosts. I have also avoided those which are linked to local customs, such as the Horngarth Ceremony of Whitby, the Goathland Plough Stots or even the popular Lyke Wake Walk. I have likewise avoided mere objects which, although part of moorland folklore, have not in themselves led to complete stories; examples are the many moorland crosses or standing stones, the unique collection of witch posts, and the curious City of Troy near Terrington.

I do not regard the harrowing account of Father Nicholas Postgate's martyrdom as folklore; that is a vital part of our turbulent religious history and I have included it in my *Murders and Mysteries from the North York Moors*. That volume includes folk stories which are not within these pages, but which contain elements of fact, such as an account of the Hand of Glory and the tale about Sarkless Kitty of Farndale; it also contains several other mysteries from the moors amongst which is the Horngarth Ceremony mentioned above. There are further accounts of folklore in my *Portrait of the North York Moors*, written as Nicholas Rhea.

In compiling this volume, I have taken the liberty of using the so-called 'novelist's licence' to occasionally weave a story around a thread of legend. Where there are several versions of one story, I have re-told that which, in my opinion, seems the most apt having regard to the available information.

It is hoped that this volume will serve as a guide to the locations of those stories which have for centuries been part of our moorland heritage.

Peter N. Walker
1989

1 Beggar's Bridge

A story of love and adventure

The beautiful and graceful Beggar's Bridge, built by Tom Ferris in 1619, spans the River Esk at Glaisdale. It has been used by the villagers for more than 370 years, a tribute to its builder. It is now almost hidden between a modern road-bridge constructed in iron and some railway arches built of local stone. The only concession to modernization is a pair of small stone bollards at each end of Beggar's Bridge to prevent weighty motor vehicles attempting to cross it. Glaisdale is the focus of other folk stories (see chapter eight), but the remarkable, romantic life of Tom Ferris deserves a chapter to itself.

Like so many moorland tales, the tale of Beggar's Bridge has produced several versions which are a fascinating mixture of fact and fiction, but there is a true story to be told. Although the passage of time has blurred the truth, we do know something about Tom Ferris. To begin with, there are several spellings of his name, including 'Ferries', 'Ferrans', 'Firris', 'Ferrers' and 'Ferris', but I shall use the one I have used since I was a child in this very village: 'Ferris'.

It is almost certain that he was born at Lastingham in 1568, the son of a moorland sheep-farmer, and at the age of fourteen he was apprenticed to a Hull ship-owner. This would have been in 1582.

During breaks in training, he did not always return to Lastingham but instead went to Egton to stay with relatives. Egton was much more convenient. Hull ships visited Whitby, only a short distance away and young Ferris probably used this method of travel between Hull and Egton.

It was while enjoying one of these breaks that he met a young woman. The opportunity may have occurred during one of the marvellous Egton fairs which attracted young people from a wide area. The annual fair lasted eight days. A charter for this had been granted in the thirteenth century to the estate owners, the de Mauleys, and a further four fairs were approved by William III. These became the famous hiring fairs – the main ones were the Martinmas Hirings held at the Feast of St Martin of Tours, 11 November, the Whitsuntide hirings in May, and the Michaelmas Hirings on St Michael's Day, 29 September. At each there was feasting, music and dancing, as well as sideshows and contests, plus the traditional hiring of farm hands and servant girls. It is almost certain that young Ferris, on leave from Hull, met the girl of his dreams at one of these fairs.

She was Agnes Richardson, the daughter of the Squire of Glaisdale, and she lived with her parents in a fine house overlooking the green at Glaisdale.

Squire Richardson was a wealthy and influential man who did not consider young Ferris a suitable match for Agnes and he expressed his dislike at their meetings. This served only to make the couple more determined to see one another, even if it was during Tom's infrequent visits to Egton.

In addition to the Squire, however, there was another problem for Tom and Agnes: the River Esk. Whenever they met, Tom had to wade across the river at Glaisdale. There was probably a set of stepping stones, but when the water was high, Tom had to wade across and when it was in flood, it was impossible to cross. Visiting Agnes was therefore a hazardous affair, but did not weaken Tom's resolve. Many was the time he arrrived at Glaisdale soaking wet, dirty and tired only to find he was not allowed to visit Agnes at her home. His difficulties were

known to the Squire; he had never forbidden Agnes to
meet the lad, merely expressed his opinion that Tom was
unsuitable. Consequently Tom's wet, filthy and unkempt
condition served only to reinforce the Squire's views. He
did not want such a scruffy individual in the house.

Tom, however, could not imagine life without his
beloved Agnes and in spite of the Squire's obvious
disapproval, he made a decision to marry Agnes. He knew
it would bring protests and even outright refusal from the
Squire, but Tom was prepared for this. Alone with Tom,
Squire Richardson refused to permit the marriage, so Tom
asked, 'Sir, if I become as wealthy as yourself, will you
then permit me to marry Agnes?'

'And will Agnes wait that long?' smiled the Squire.

'She will,' said Tom with confidence.

'Then, and only then, will I give my consent,' said
Richardson. 'But until then, you must meet no more.'

Faced with this ultimatum, Tom knew he must explain
things to Agnes, but the Squire allowed no opportunity. In
his view, the parting must be swift and final. Agnes and
Tom had previously discussed marriage and she knew
that Tom was going to approach her father, she had no
idea, however, of his blunt but conditional refusal.
Although the lovers could not meet, they did have a
signalling system,. Agnes' house was on the edge of the
moor at Glaisdale and occupied an elevated position with
extensive views across the Esk Valley towards Egton.
From time to time when the Squire and his wife were
away, Agnes would place a light in her bedroom window
and this was the signal for Tom to trek to Glaisdale. The
couple would walk in the romantic glens of Arncliffe
Wood, with Tom telling her glowing stories of his
seafaring life.

He told her of pirates and foreign countries, of people of
all colours and customs, of fascinating towns and cities
and of jungles and deserts. He recounted wonderful
stories from that time, in 1586, when he had joined the
British fleet under Sir Francis Drake; how they had sailed
to the West Indies and how Drake was such a superb

leader of men, such a brave and uncompromising man at sea ...

With his tales, Tom had convinced Agnes that he *would* become rich and that he would marry her ... but now he was unable to meet Agnes with news of her father's embargo on their meetings. He returned in sorrow to his uncle's home at Egton and then, on 7 May 1588, he received an urgent message. Tomorrow he must travel in haste to Whitby to join a ship bound for Hull; there he would rejoin Sir Francis Drake who was amassing a fleet of ships which were needed to fight for Queen Elizabeth I and England. Somehow, Tom had to tell Agnes of his unexpected development and, happily, that evening he saw the light in her window. It meant they could meet. Tonight she would be waiting for him with a hot meal, a bottle of her father's finest wine and a roaring fire ...

When he reached the river at Glaisdale, however, it was in flood. There had been a fierce storm on the moors over Westerdale and a flash-flood had filled the Esk with swirling, muddy water. It had overflowed its banks and was several feet above its normal level, roaring through the dale with a noise like thunder. Tree trunks and dead sheep were being carried along like corks; any man caught in that raging torrent would be swept to certain death. In the darkness of that stormy May night Tom could not say farewell to Agnes, and tomorrow there would be no further opportunity. In her house on the hill, a mile's walk from the riverside, Agnes would never know of this sudden flood. For a long time, Tom waited for the waters to recede, but it would take hours for this to happen.

To attempt to wade would be fatal; even a cart-horse would be swept off its feet in that torrent and so, with a heavy heart, Tom Ferris turned his back on Glaisdale and returned to Egton. He would have to sail without seeing Agnes; it would seem as though he had forsaken her and this would reinforce her father's opinion of him.

At dawn next morning, 8 May 1588, he boarded a ship at Whitby to learn rumours of an impending battle. Ten days later, on 18 May 1588, an Armada of 130 vessels sailed from Spain to invade England. It bore 7,000 sailors and 17,000 soldiers, but bad weather forced it to take shelter in Corunna Harbour, Spain; there were problems with food and fresh water and other military matters to resolve, so the final sailing of the Armada was delayed until July. It was heading for England and was sighted off the Lizard, Cornwall, on 19 July 1588.

Tom Ferris fought alongside Sir Francis Drake, the commander-in-chief, and others like Sir John Hawkins, Sir Martin Frobisher and Lord Howard. The rest is history – Drake's superb tactics enabled the English to beat the Spanish Armada and the bravery of Tom Ferris during that battle won him the personal compliments of Sir Francis. Afterwards, Drake invited Tom to join him on other expeditions and he did so. They travelled the seas where Tom engaged in piracy. He seized many foreign ships and in 1592, still only twenty-four years old, he sailed triumphantly into London with a captured foreign vessel.

By selling it he increased the fortune he had earned through his sea-faring exploits, and upon his return he travelled immediately to Glaisdale to claim the hand of Agnes Richardson.

It was a different Tom Ferris who now arrived at the Squire's fine home. He was now a man of culture and wealth and he was dressed in fine clothes and rode a superb horse. The Squire, a man of his word, gave his ready consent for Agnes had waited all those turbulent years. Although no record of the marriage exists, it is known that they did marry, either at Glaisdale which then had a chapel as part of Danby parish, or at Danby itself, the parent church. Afterwards, Mr and Mrs Tom Ferris settled in Hull where he established a very successful shipping company. He became a substantial businessman soon afterwards and in 1614, aged forty-six he became Sheriff of Hull. Had Squire Richardson lived to witness his success, he would have been proud of his son-in-law.

Sadly in 1618, Agnes died. Tom was distraught, and in his sorrow, absorbed himself in civic duties. As he continued to increase his fortune and achieve further civic success, he recalled that terrible night in May 1588, thirty years earlier, when he could not cross the River Esk to say farewell to his Agnes. He decided to build a suitable monument to her memory and so arranged for the construction of the bridge which is now called Beggar's Bridge. It was finished in 1619 and bears that date and Tom's initials on a top stone in one parapet.

In 1620, Tom became Lord Mayor of Hull and he was also chosen three times to be the honorary head of Trinity House in Hull, which is the training centre for seafaring people. He was a man of great wealth and used his money for several gifts to the people of the North York Moors – he gave to Trinity House his estate known as Whitefriars Estate which still provides an income and, in 1620, in memory of his happy childhood at Lastingham, he paid for the re-roofing of Lastingham church and built a new school for the village.

After Beggar's Bridge had been built, but also in 1620, Tom re-married and continued his benevolent work in Hull where he died in 1631 aged sixty-three. He is buried in Holy Trinity Church, Hull, where an inscription said, 'Here lieth the body of the Worshipful Thomas Ferris, master and mariner, once Mayor of this town who departed this life in the true faith of Christ, Anno Dom., 1631. Quod sum fueris.'

In his will, he left an income of £6.13s. 4d. (£6.66) to be paid annually to Danby's priest in whose parish Glaisdale was situated and a further sum of £2 for the upkeep of Glaisdale's chapel, now Glaisdale parish church of St Thomas. A plaque in Danby church commemorates this gift and, in Glaisdale church, there is also a portrait of Tom Ferris. It is a copy of one which hangs in Trinity House, Hull, and the Warden has since presented to Glaisdale church a silver communion set inscribed to the memory of Tom Ferris.

The most remarkable tribute to him, however, is Beggar's Bridge which continues to span the Esk at Glaisdale. In 1930, a score of bridges across the Esk were washed away in a flood of the kind that had prevented Tom from bidding farewell to Agnes, but his bridge, then more than 300 years old, survived. It was almost as if those ancient stones were saying to the world that no flood would ever again prevent the meeting of true lovers.

So who owns Beggar's Bridge now? In the 1980s, it became in need of urgent repair and, as no one came forward to claim responsibility, it was taken into the care of the North York Moors National Park authority.

2   Castleton

Young Ralph, Old Ralph, Fat Betty and Margery

Castleton was once the largest village in Eskdale, being a trading centre with a thriving market and a busy railway station. Reminders of its past bustling role are in the form of a disused weavers' mill and the closure of the Robin Hood and Little John Inn which bore a sign saying, 'Kind gentlemen and yeoman good, call in and drink with Robin Hood. If Robin be not at home, step in and drink with Little John.'

Today, it is a peaceful village lined with sturdy, dark stone, terraced houses under blue slate roofs; in many ways, it is a typical moorland village for its houses present the Yorkshire image of strength and durability. The church of St George and St Michael was built in the 1920s and contains a lot of oak woodwork, much of it bearing the mouse trademark from Robert Thompson of Kilburn near Thirsk. There is an ancient history to the district, as is shown by the numerous archaeological remains on the moors, especially those of the Bronze Age. In 1937, a body was discovered 1,400 feet above sea-level at Loose Howe. It was in a coffin fashioned from two dug-out boats made from a tree-trunk. Beside the body was a bronze dagger, thought to have been made around 3,000 years ago. It was one of the most important Bronze Age burials to be found in the North of England.

As the name suggests, there was once a castle here; it was a Norman motte-castle built originally of wood with three moats, although by around 1160 there were some stone structures on the site. It overlooked the Esk valley, with its north-facing wall being thirteen feet thick, but it fell into disuse as the influence of nearby Danby Castle increased. Today, the village overlooks the site of its former castle which was close to the present church.

There are picturesque views from the moors above Castleton and a warm welcome from the remote Lion Inn on Blakey Moor at the side of the road to Hutton-le-Hole. Not far from this inn was a cockpit which hosted fights between teams from the Stokesley and Guisborough areas and others from Pickering and Kirkbymoorside. Many a 'battle-royal' has been fought here before hundreds of competitors and spectators; the cockpit was last used in 1760.

High on the moors between Castleton and Rosedale, very close to the Lion Inn, stands a nine-foot-tall, slender stone cross which is the symbol of the North York Moors National Park. It is on the side of the Hutton-le-Hole to Castleton road close to the junctions with both the Rosedale road and the Westerdale road. The cross is widely known as 'Ralph's Cross' but its correct name is 'Young Ralph'. Old Ralph, a shorter stone standing at a shade less than five feet high, stands a couple of hundred yards across the moors to the west while nearby are two ladylike stones known as Fat Betty and the Margery Stone.

There are hundreds of stone crosses, standing stones and waymarkers on these moors; indeed, for such a compact area, this is probably England's largest assembly of such stones and crosses. There are stories concerning many of them, but we are concerned here with the legend surrounding Young Ralph, Old Ralph, Fat Betty and the Margery Stone. They are closely grouped on this remote moorland spot. In addition to Old and Young Ralph, Fat Betty is a carved piece of rock which is roughly square-shaped with a rounded head; she is painted white and is sometimes called 'White Cross'. She stands a little way down the road to Rosedale while the Margery Stone, tall, thin and oblong-shaped, is beside the Hutton-le-Hole road a short way from Young Ralph. These four intriguing stones are all within half a mile of one another, so what is their story?

There are differing accounts of the association between these stones, but the following is perhaps the most durable!

Many years ago, a group of Cistercian nuns, known as the 'White Ladies' from the colour of their habits, formed a small nunnery in Rosedale. The year was 1158 and it became known as Rosedale Priory. Memories live on in the name of the village – which is called Rosedale Abbey – a slight misnomer, although some remnants of the former priory can be seen. These are a short tower and staircase near the church of St Lawrence and a curious sundial on the end of a nearby building, but much of the stone from the ruins was used in many new buildings in Rosedale, especially during last century's iron-ore boom.

As the nuns were establishing themselves in Rosedale, so another community was being created at Baysdale Abbey, some nine miles across the moors to the north-west. These were also Cistercian nuns. Their first nunnery had been at Hutton Low Cross near Guisborough. Founded there in 1162, it moved to a village called Thorpe which is now called Nunthorpe in their honour, and they later moved deeper into the moors to Baysdale, then spelt 'Basedale'. Baysdale is near Kildale and remains a remote and peaceful valley. The abbey was founded here around 1200 and contained only a dozen nuns.

The two Cistercian communities therefore lived nearby, albeit separated by a block of high, rugged and inhospitable moorland. The Rosedale nuns were not finding life very easy; their way of life made the local people wary of them and there was even some antagonism. Fortunately, they had one staunch supporter in an old man called Ralph who acted as a general handyman and lay worker for the nuns. One of his tasks was to act as a moorland guide should the nuns ever travel from their lovely valley of Rosedale. Such an occasion did occur when a religious dispute affected the two nunneries.

It involved the interpretation of the rules of their way of life, and so it was decided that a learned representative of each community should meet to resolve the matter. The two selected nuns decided to rendezvous midway between the two nunneries. The ideal place was a lofty moorland site near the concourse of several highways and tracks: the point where Old Ralph now stands.

Rosedale Priory was to be represented by Sister Elizabeth and Baysdale Abbey was to send Sister Margery. Sister Elizabeth was fortunate because she was to be accompanied on this long trek by her faithful servant, old Ralph, but Sister Margery, coming in the opposite direction, travelled alone. It seems the weather was favourable during the long walk from Rosedale, although we are not told what it was like on the route from Baysdale.

When Sister Elizabeth and old Ralph arrived at the rendezvous point, there was no sign of Sister Margery. From there, they could see across the moors and deep into Eskdale, but they could not see the oncoming nun. In her white robes, she should have been clearly visible against the heather. They decided they must await her arrival, however long it took. As they waited on the heights, however, with Elizabeth seated on a larger rock to rest her weary feet, a thick and chilling fog suddenly descended. On the moors, these are known as roaks; they are dense and cold, and within minutes can obliterate everything from view.

The faithful Ralph now had a problem. He decided the best thing was to seek Margery while leaving Elizabeth safe on the large stone. If she did not stray, she would be safe until the roak lifted, being well wrapped in her thick robes. She had brought some refreshments too. She agreed, and so Ralph went to find Sister Margery.

He relied on his own deep knowledge of the moors and his skill at following sheep tracks and other natural routes. He would maintain contact by shouting from time to time. So off went the brave old Ralph.

As he vanished into the heavy white mist, Sister Elizabeth felt worried in case he became lost, or if he fell and injured himself, and so occupied herself by praying for him. She prayed with all her heart that the roak might lift and clear the view. She could hear Ralph shouting Margery's name, his voice sounding so faint in the thick mist and so soft owing to the distance he had covered. Sometimes he called her name and she shouted back to give reassurance, but her voice was not so strong and it is probable that he never heard her. Other than Ralph's occasional call, there was not a sound on those moors. The roak had deadened all noise: there was no song from the skylark, no bleating of the sheep, no chattering of the grouse, only a sombre, dampening silence.

Eventually Ralph's voice ceased. No longer could his faint calls be heard through the dense mist and she feared the worst. She worried that he had injured himself, or that the aged man had died in his brave attempt to help; so she prayed even harder, both for Ralph's safety and for the awful mist to rise. She prayed also for Sister Margery, lost somewhere on her trek from Baysdale, but she did not stray from her sanctuary on the rock.

Then the roak lifted. As suddenly as it had appeared it evaporated in the afternoon sun and the moors were bathed in the bright light of day. She watched in delight as the rolling clouds swept along the heather, rising into the sky to evaporate like steam from a boiling fish.

Elizabeth could now hear Ralph's voice once more. She stood on the high stone and there she could see him, only half a mile away; and half a mile in the other direction, was the white robed figure of Sister Margery. On meeting, the two nuns embraced and wept with relief, learning that poor old Ralph had shouted until he was hoarse in his efforts to locate them. In the fog, Margery had arrived at what she had thought was the rendezvous stone, but now realized it was the wrong one. She had completed her journey after Ralph's voice had disappeared.

They could now enjoy the food they had brought, and then have their important discussions. Old Ralph was so relieved that, as the two nuns talked, he named each stone and recorded their positions. He called one 'the White Cross' in honour of Sister Elizabeth and her white robes, although later generations nicknamed it 'Fat Betty'. That stone is white to this day, but the name is due to the dimensions of the rock, not the size of Sister Elizabeth! The Margery Stone, a rough, unhewn slab of rock, acts as a guide to travellers for it is a way marker for those who undertake the forty-mile Lyke Wake Walk across these heights, and it also serves as a rendezvous point for support parties. It is sometimes called 'Margery Bradley' or simply 'Old Margery'.

Old Ralph continues to stand on his elevated piece of moorland as he has for centuries past, but Young Ralph is a modern arrival. He dates only to around the eighteenth century, being a replica of a much earlier cross; it is known that a cross called 'Crux Radulphi', stood here and served as a boundary stone in the thirteenth century. So Young Ralph is something of an intruder into this trio, but he does his best to assist poor travellers. It is said that, after a traveller died from exhaustion here, a sympathetic farmer erected Young Ralph on the site and ordered that a hollow be made in the top so that those who could afford it could place money or food for the benefit of needy travellers. That hollow is still there; even now, it sometimes contains coins which are for the use of those in need. The cross has twice been damaged by people seeking these coins, and in 1984 it was savagely and senselessly vandalized but now stands proud and repaired. Old Ralph would be proud of his young namesake.

Old Ralph, Margery and Fat Betty are separated from one another by a few hundred yards of moorland, and the legend is that if they ever get together, then Ralph will marry Betty! Another tale is that if three kings ever meet one another at Old Ralph, then the world will come to an end.

3 Crayke

A saint and a sinner

The village of Crayke, with its assorted houses clinging to the slopes of a steep mound in the Vale of York, lies a few miles to the south of the North York Moors. It is close enough, however, to justify inclusion in this volume if only through its association with St Cuthbert of Durham. The village inn bears the odd name of 'The Durham Ox', an indication of Crayke's ancient links with County Durham whose boundaries are many miles to the north. Crayke also has links, however, with a Scandinavian epic.

There is a lot of history here as testified by its castle, which at the time of writing (1989) is a hotel. It is known that there was a fortress or timber castle here in Saxon times, for the village occupies a strategic site with commanding views across the plain below. In the twelfth century, the Normans built a motte-and-bailey castle, probably on the site of its Saxon predecessor. Parts of the present castle date to that time, although it was virtually rebuilt during extensions in the fifteenth century. Some accounts for an extension of its stables in 1441 record the changes of that time; the portion built in 1441 is still occupied. The castle and the surrounding estate later became the property of the Bishops of Durham and at least five reigning sovereigns stayed here.

The Bishops of Durham always spent part of their year at the castle too and it remained in their hands until the time of Bishop Van Mildert (1826-39). Wishing to purchase an estate closer to Durham, he sold Crayke Castle to a Mr J.R. Thompson. It has been in private hands since that time and is not open to the public, except in its present role as a hotel.

The present church of St Cuthbert was 'modernized' as long ago as the fifteenth century and is an impressive sight with its battlements and imposing tower. Some ancient stones have been incorporated, including the arms of an eighth-century Anglo-Saxon cross; the chancel screen was restored in the fifteenth century and the canopied pulpit dates to 1637.

One of Crayke's famous sons was William Ralph Inge (1860-1954) who was Dean of St Paul's in London from 1911 until 1934. Widely known as Dean Inge, he wrote books on his religion and was known for his interest in mysticism.

Crayke's most famous visitor, however, both in life and in death, was St Cuthbert. An Englishman from Northumbria, he was renowned for his total devotion to God and his Church. He was both an intellectual and a practical man, a rare combination, and is described as a man of extraordinary charm. Born around AD 634, Cuthbert died on the Northumbrian Farne Islands in AD 687. He was buried on 20 March which is now his feast day. When Cuthbert's grave was opened eleven years later, the body was still fresh and had not decomposed. The body was re-interred as news of this miracle spread and a shrine was established at the grave.

In AD 793, however, the Vikings raided the Farne Islands and the monks fled but returned later to find the shrine of St Cuthbert had been spared. A later raid was more threatening; this time, to avoid its desecration by the marauders, the monks took with them the inviolate body of St Cuthbert as they fled. Into the coffin, they placed other treasures, including the bones of St Aidan, then set off for the mainland.

For the next seven years, they roamed the north of England, the coffin being carried by seven trusted men. No one else was allowed even to touch the coffin and they

managed to keep their holy relic safe from the Vikings and
other raiders. They were supported by donations of food,
clothing and money as they roamed. Finally, in AD 883,
they settled at Chester-le-Street in County Durham and
remained there for over 100 years until a new scare by
more marauding Danes sent them once more on their
journeying with Cuthbert's body. On this occasion, they
reached as far south as Ripon and Crayke. For four
months, the body of St Cuthbert was hidden in Crayke; it
never returned to Chester-le-Street but eventually found
peace in Durham.

The precise location of that Crayke resting place is of
interest because in AD 685, two years before Cuthbert's
death, he was given by King Egfridus, the 'the town of
Crayke and three miles around it' (*tria in circuito ipsius
villae miliaria*).

The King did this so that Cuthbert would own a place of
rest on his journeys to and from York and it seems that
Cuthbert made good use of his gift to found a monastery.
A hermit called Etha died here in AD 767, but it is claimed
that this monastery led to the foundation of the present
church in Crayke. In other words, Crayke church is
actually dedicated to its founder, not its patron saint.

This being so, it seems that the church, or that part of it
which then existed, was a most suitable place for the
concealment of Cuthbert's body during its terrible travels.
By tradition, every place that the body rested became part
of the County of Durham and so the village of Crayke,
although within the North Riding of Yorkshire, then
belonged to the Palatine County of Durham. It remained a
part of Durham until 1844 when an Act of Parliament
restored it to Yorkshire.

Cuthbert's body was re-examined in 1104 when a start
was made on the new cathedral at Durham; it was still in
perfect condition and the body was even flexible. Poor
Cuthbert was not allowed to rest even then – when Henry
VIII's commissioners came to Durham in 1537 as part of
Henry's destruction of the monasteries, the coffin of St
Cuthbert was again opened. The body was still in perfect

condition with no sign of decay and it was placed in the inner vestry until the King's wishes for its disposal became known.

It is said that it was later re-buried under the present shrine, but is this so? After all that St Cuthbert's body had tolerated since death, would the devoted monks risk harm to those sacred remains by leaving them to the whim of the reforming vandal, Henry VIII? A hint of some deception arises through a further disturbance to the saint's coffin in 1827. This time when St Cuthbert's coffin was opened, the body it contained had decayed, although the vestments and other relics remained. Legend says the shrine in Durham Cathedral is not the true burial place of St Cuthbert – one account says that, due to the risks attached to Catholic relics and saints during Henry VIII's Reformation, the body was concealed, perhaps within the secret confines of Durham Cathedral and that another body occupies his supposed grave. Or might St Cuthbert lie in peace at his old monastery at Crayke? Wherever the saint rests, that place was known only to three Benedictine monks who have always passed on the secret to three successors. The nearest community of Benedictine monks is that at Ampleforth Abbey, some six miles from Crayke. Do they know the secret of St Cuthbert? Legend says the skeletal remains found in 1827 are not those of the saint, but of a substituted body. However, history tells us that St Cuthbert is now at rest in Durham Cathderal and it must be said that the shrine does have a most awesome atmosphere.

There is another story of Crayke, however. This one spans the North Sea and concerns a cruel battle between two kings, one of whom is a major folk hero of Scandinavia. Like the story of St Cuthbert, it dates to around the seventh/ninth centuries when the village was known as Crec. The fortress existed on the hill where the castle now stands, and Crayke was still in the Saxon kingdom of Deira.

The time of the tale which follows was after St

Cuthbert's death. Indeed, the King of Northumbria, called Aella, might well have confiscated Crayke's ancient castle as news of Cuthbert's death reached the village. If the saint was dead, who could prevent him taking Crayke? King Aella lived here for a time, converting the castle to his own needs – complete with underground dungeons.

At the same time, there lived in the Danish islands, a feared and famous king called Ragnar Lodbrok. He features widely in Scandinavian folklore and poetry where he is acclaimed a brave, upstanding and conquering hero. His queen, Austaga, was a shepherdess who was known for both her beauty and her qualities as a singer; she had worked in the mountains of Norway before winning the heart of the renowned Ragnar.

In fact, there were two Scandinavian heroes of this name, Ragnar Lodbrok who died in AD 794 and a later one who led invasions of France and England in the ninth century. It is not certain which decided to invade England. However, the story tells us that Ragnar equipped himself with two superb warships, the biggest and best that had ever been built in Denmark.

He recruited an army of very trusty men, then decided to invade England. He sailed across the North Sea towards Northumbria where he landed somewhere close to Bamburgh. Aella was elsewhere at the time, working in the southern area of his kingdom near York, so the invading Ragnar devastated the immediate vicinity. He took to burning farmsteads and crops, looting the villages, raping the women and girls and killing the domestic animals of the Northumbrian folk. There was no one to halt him, but the news did reach Aella. Aella was determined that no invading Dane would treat the subjects of his Kingdom in such a manner and soon the two confronted one another, each with their armies.

Aella's men were equal to the task and annihilated the Danes in a shocking and bloody battle. But Ragnar was not killed – Aella managed to take him prisoner and many then said that this was indeed a fate worse than military death. Aella was noted for his cruelty; he spared no one who dared to cross him, he had no compassion for his enemies and no respect for the royal rank of his prisoner. He escorted Ragnar to Crayke Castle and decided to make an example of him. After what he was going to do to Ragnar, no more would the Vikings and Northmen dare to invade Northumbria ...

At Crayke Castle, Aella had a particularly deep and evil dungeon; it was black and damp and was filled with poisonous snakes and evil reptiles of every kind. He kept that dungeon as a means of torture and death for his enemies. The only entrance was a hole at the top and prisoners were lowered into the depths by means of a rope which was secured to a ring so that they could be raised and lowered to the amusement of the gloating Aella. This was Ragnar's fate.

Stripped of all his clothes, and lashed at the hands and feet, he was lowered at the end of a rope and vanished into the blackness of that awful place. From time to time, he was dragged back to the surface to the glee of his tormentor who taunted him cruelly and asked him to beg for mercy. But Ragnar was no coward. He refused to plead for forgiveness nor did he capitulate to Aella; instead, he retaliated by cursing his captor and threatening him with death from his avenging sons. We are not told how long this torture continued, but we are told that further dangerous reptiles and poisonous snakes were added to that bleak dungeon. Time and time again, Ragnar was hauled to the surface where he responded only by cursing and threatening Aella even though he was weak from lack of food and sleep, and severely bitten by the reptiles.

Finally, with Ragnar on the point of collapse, he was dragged for the final time to the opening of his dungeon and asked to beg for mercy. He refused yet again, saying, 'Aella, upon my death, my kinsmen shall sail from Denmark, they will slay you and your subjects, they will avenge my death in a most terrible manner, and at the tables in the banqueting halls of Valhalla, they shall drink a toast to Odin from your skull.'

With that, he was lowered for the last time into the pit of

poisonous snakes. So died a famous Scandinavian warrior and king.

His death song, *Lodbrokar-quida,* became a Scandinavian epic; his three sons, Hinga, Hubba and Bruen, sailed from Denmark to avenge his death. They came up the Humber, laid siege to York and defeated Aella, his allies and their armies. One account suggests that Aella was captured alive and flayed to death, but his Kingdom of Northumbria was taken over by the invading Danes.

4 Egton

The barguest of Egton

Egton stands on a hill overlooking the Esk Valley some seven miles from Whitby and is about a mile and a half from the A171. Clustered around a couple of inns and a church, it is a small community which has often attracted artists; several have made their homes here to capture the beauty of the moors and the Esk Valley.

In 1070, the village was given to Nigel Fossard by William the Conqueror. The name is recorded in the Domesday Book as 'Egetune', meaning town of oaks, for the valley below was once heavily wooded with oaks; it was such a delightful place that William the Conqueror's blacksmith left him at York to settle at Egton! The village is noted for the Egton Horse and Agricultural Society which stages an annual show in August. It is one of the largest in this part of England and its forerunners can be traced back to the thirteenth century.

In the thirteenth century, the estate owners, the de Mauleys, obtained a market charter which allowed an annual fair lasting eight days. Later, another charter granted by William III allowed the holding of four further fairs and in time these became the traditional hiring fairs. The farmers and farm workers would visit the fairs during their annual holidays.

It was during these fairs that farmers selected their workers for the coming year, so hopeful lads and lasses would congregate as the farmers and their wives examined them. If any lad or lass was taken on, the deal would be sealed by the farmer handing over a 'fastning penny' or God's penny which was their way of saying that agreement had been reached. The coin could be a penny or indeed a coin of any value. Hiring fairs ended with the Agricultural Wages Act of 1924.

Beautifully situated in the valley about a mile from Egton is Egton Bridge, one of Yorkshire's prettiest villages. It is one of England's most famous Roman Catholic parishes, being known as 'the village missed by the Reformation'. It is the birthplace of Father Nicholas Postgate, the Martyr of the Moors, who was executed at York at the age of eighty-two in 1679, for baptizing a child into the Catholic faith. The huge church of St Hedda, built in 1866, dominates the village and halfway between Egton and Egton Bridge is the mass house where Father Postgate celebrated mass in secret. (For a fuller account of his life and work, see *Murders and Mysteries from the North York Moors* by Peter N. Walker, published by Robert Hale.)

In Egton Bridge, the Egton Bridge Old Gooseberry Society, formed in 1800, holds its annual gooseberry show on the first Tuesday in August. In 1982, the world record for the heaviest gooseberry was achieved at this show.

Halfway up the hill between the two Egtons is St Hilda's Anglican church built in 1878-9, parts of which have been formed from the former church on this site. The first was built around 1349, and associated with that earlier church there is a weird story.

It concerns a barguest. A barguest was a fearsome apparition which appeared shortly before the death of a local person. It was therefore a herald of death, but its appearance varied widely. There are barguests which have the form of huge animals, such as: black dogs, white cats, calves, pigs, goats, large rabbits, and other evil creatures which took the form of domestic animals. Whatever their appearance, they were never mistaken for ordinary domestic beasts because they had huge, saucer-like eyes, and feet which left no mark in the earth. There are several accounts of barguests throughout the north-east of England, and one of their distinguishing features is their ghastly howling. They supposedly issue terrifying roars or shrieks. There is a saying 'To roar like a barguest', which indicates a frightening sound.

The word is said to come from the German 'berg-geist' which means mountain demon or 'bahrgeist', the spirit of the bier; in the north of England, the word is variously spelt as 'bargest', 'bierguest', 'barguest', 'bahrgeist' or 'boguest'. On the Continent, a similar creature is called a 'kirkgrim'; this was the ghost of a creature such as a lamb or a dog which had been buried alive under the foundations of a church to give strength and durability to the building. Some witnesses claim to have seen these kirkgrims before the death of a loved one.

In parts of West Yorkshire, a similar creature was called a 'padfoot'; this was a creature about the size of a donkey. It had long black shaggy hair, eyes like saucers and it followed travellers at night as it uttered its ghastly roar. This was also said to presage death and seems to be another name for the barguest or kirkgrim.

In the case of the Egton Barguest, a man was walking up the hill late one evening when the barguest confronted him close to where St Hilda's Church now stands. He knew it was a 'bier ghost', as he called it, and he fled from its awful attentions as it howled and chased him through the night. He described it as, 'nowt like man nor beast, a greeat awful creeature with een like saucers and nut a morsel o' noise frev its feet ...'.

5 Farndale

The hob that flitted

The remoteness of Farndale has long isolated this beautiful dale from the world. It is a long narrow valley with steep sides and is almost completely surrounded by open moorland. Access is gained through either Kirkbymoorside or Hutton-le-Hole, each in themselves interesting places, while another dramatic route is the sharp descent from Blakey Rigg, off the Hutton-le-Hole to Castleton road.

In the springtime, the banks of the River Dove are smothered with masses of wild daffodils. Millions extend in colourful profusion for six or seven miles along the riverside. There are several varieties and these are the true wild daffodils which are native to Britain. The reason for their presence in such huge numbers is because the low-lying damp pastures provide precisely the right elements for their continuing growth. They do grow in other dales, but nowhere in such profusion. Yorkshire people call them Lenten Lilies for they bloom around Easter-time, and both plants and bulbs are protected by law. In 1953, the North Riding County Council designated 2,000 acres of Farndale as a local nature reserve.

Farndale's name probably comes from the Gaelic 'fearna' which has links with alders which flourish along the banks of the River Dove, but there is no village called 'Farndale'. The name applies to the entire dale which contains three hamlets: Church Houses, Low Mill and

Lowna, each some distance apart. The dale features a scattering of farmhouses and cottages, among them many old cruck houses and thatched buildings. Some have disappeared within the last ten or fifteen years, but several do remain and they are carefully maintained.

The very isolation of Farndale has given rise to many associated legends and myths and the dale is rich with tales of witchcraft and superstition. I have included two strong Farndale stories in my *Murders and Mysteries from the North York Moors* (the story of Sarkless Kitty, and the Mystery Bones of Middle Head), but there are others, some of which I will include in this volume.

One concerns a well-known witch who lived near Danby. She was called Nan Hardwicke and was known to hide among the heather as she cast her spells, but the local lads would flush her out with hounds then chase her. But, so the story says, they never caught her. The reason was that she could transform herself into a hare and so escape any dog. Nan's links with Farndale were through a relation who lived at Lowna, one of the Farndale hamlets. Nan would regularly travel to Lowna to visit this relative, although we are told she was rarely welcomed.

People would often puzzle over Nan's ability to travel so quickly across the moors between Danby and Lowna, and the answer was that she changed into a hare for the journey. (See the chapter on Glaisdale for further accounts of witch hares.)

The following story shows how she exercised her witchcraft during one of these visits. She had travelled the moors to visit Lowna because the daughter of her cousin was being married that day. Although not specifically invited due to her peculiar habits and personality' Nan did make the journey and arrived at Lowna just after the bridal procession had returned from the church. It was the custom then, among the dales families, for long-distance travellers to stay the night in the family home, and Nan, having walked the ten miles or so from Danby across the remote and inhospitable moors, expected to be given a bed. Every bed was full, however, some with more than one sleeper. Nan was told there was no room. It seemed she would have to walk all the way back to Danby unless she camped in a barn or loft. A kindly bridesmaid, however, came to the rescue. She heard of Nan's plight and said, 'I'll take Nan home with me, she can share my bed.'

At this offer, the bride, not realizing Nan was within hearing distance, said, 'I know she's a relation of mine, but I'd never have that filthy old thing in my house!'

Nan heard this retort and swung around to confront the girl, saying, 'No, but you'd sleep with him!', pointing to the bridegroom with her walking stick. Her loud voice caused the assembled guests to fall silent and then, with an ominous tone to her voice, Nan said,

'Ah've let tha be wedded, but Ah'll stop tha being bedded!'

with that she stalked out of the celebrations. Everyone ignored the remark, thinking it was merely the retort of a silly old woman, and they settled down to enjoy the food and drink. The bridesmaids were charming and the lads were boisterous in their happiness, until it was time for the bride and groom to retire to bed.

As was the custom, the bride climbed the stairs some time before the groom and settled in her wedding bed to await her new husband. One of the bridesmaids, the sister of the groom, whispered to him that it was no use him trying to join his bride by climbing the stairs. The lads had plotted to prevent him gaining the bedroom, a common piece of fun at such an event. They intended to keep him from his bride for the entire night.

On such occasions, though, the bridesmaids always tried to frustrate those attempts by their own scheming and in this case, they had worked out a plan with the bride. They had organized a game of blind man's bluff among the guests and, as the eager bride waited in her bedroom, the game got underway. All the men were blindfolded and all the girls carried lighted candles. The men had to circle the room as the music played, and when it stopped they had to remove their masks and 'in the dark, kiss the girl they loved the best'.

And so, as the music sounded, the men toured the room, and then, as one of the bridesmaids called, 'Now kiss the girl you love the best', all the girls blew out their candles. In the darkness and happy confusion that followed, the bridegroom slipped out of the room and, instead of using the staircase to his bride's room, he rushed outside to where the bridesmaids had placed a ladder to her window. It was not quite long enough for him to climb in through the window, and so the girls had lashed a towel to the window frame and it dangled down the wall for him to use in the final climb. Hurriedly, he climbed the ladder and was in the act of preparing to haul himself up the final few feet with the aid of the towel, when the revellers realized what was happening. One of them dashed outside, saw the groom aloft and immediately knocked the ladder away. The unfortunate groom fell to the ground and broke his leg. Old Nan's curse had come true and enhanced her reputation as a witch.

Another Farndale witch story involved a woman who could turn herself into a black dog. A farmer who lived near Church Houses noticed that whenever a certain black bitch approached his cowshed, one of his cows became ill. In some cases, the cow even died, and such a death was a disaster for any working farmer. The poor man became very concerned that it might be a local witch and sought advice from a wise man.

The wise man said that the black dog clearly was a witch who was using the form of a dog for her nefarious activities. He told him that, over the centuries, some witches had possessed the ability to turn themselves into animals such as wolves, hares, bears, greyhounds, cats or other beasts. This was a form of lycanthropy, the process by which a man turned into a werewolf ...

The farmer was told that the only way to rid himself of this witch was to shoot it with a silver bullet. No other weapon would kill a witch in animal form. The farmer therefore made himself some silver bullets from old coins and settled down to await the black bitch. It arrived one night and tried to gain entry to some calves' pens, but

failed. He was in time to see it slinking from the premises
and in the darkness he managed to aim his gun at the dog.
He fired and scored a hit, but the dog was not killed;
instead, it howled horribly and fled into the night. Next
morning, the farmer called at the home of a local witch and
found her in bed with severe gunshot wounds in her hind-
quarters. No more were his cows troubled by that black dog.

Some two or three centuries ago, there were several
witches in the Farndale area, including Aud Nan Scaife o'
Spaunton Moor who used a magical cube, Aud Mother
Migg o' Cropton who used a crystal, Aud Esther Mudd o'
Rosedale who used the evil eye and Aud Peggy Devell o'
Hutton-le-Hole who used a magic book.

Farndale is also known far and wide for its hob. High on
the moors to the east of the dale, between Low Mill and
Lowna, there is a rocky outcrop known as 'Obtrusch' or
'Hob Thrush'. There are many other locations around the
moors with the word 'Hob' as a prefix or suffix, and this
location reminds us of the famous tale of the Farndale
Hob.
    Like the other hobs, he was an elf-like fellow with long,
shaggy hair which covered his entire body. And, like the
others, he worked on a farm, in this case one worked by
Jonathan Gray, who was very industrious. The hob had
attached himself to the farm when Jonathan's grandfather
lived there, some accounts stating the hob had arrived
soon after a fearsome snowstorm during which one of the
farm workers had died. The hob had voluntarily replaced
that worker and since then had aided each successive
generation of the Gray family.
    The hob worked hard all the time, shearing sheep,
leading hay, mowing, tending the animals, tidying the
premises and doing a host of routine tasks which were
always necessary. No-one ever saw him at work for he
worked in secret, and the only reward sought by the hob
was a night jug of cream. This had to be left in the barn at
the end of each day, and he would enjoy it in silence, quite
content with his own company and never seeking the

companionship of humans. Year in and year out, therefore, he worked for the Gray family and when Jonathan married, his wife accepted the presence of the hob and continued to reward him with his jug of cream.

Jonathan prospered and his farm was considered one of the best in Farndale, for it was highly efficient and immaculately kept. Tragedy was soon to follow, however, when Jonathan's young wife died. For a time, he worked alone, albeit aided by the unseen hob who supported him so well during his sadness; but Jonathan needed a wife and so, after a suitable period of mourning, he remarried.

His new wife, however, was mean with money. When Jonathan explained the reason for placing a jug of best cream in the barn each night, to be used by an unseen creature, his wife objected. She regarded it as a waste of money, even though it had continued for generations. Jonathan insisted that it was necessary, but one night his wife, unbeknown to him, exchanged the cream for a jug of skimmed milk.

At that stage, the hob stopped work. Instead of leaving, he became mischievous and things started to go wrong about the farm. The cheese always turned sour, foxes attacked the hens and geese, cattle became sick and the crops failed; worse still, some kind of evil poltergeist began to haunt the farmhouse and it terrified the servants and labourers who lived there. No one would work for Jonathan any more. In a matter of months, his prosperous farm began to ail and he was reduced from being a very successful businessman to a mere shadow of his former self. He was ill, he could not sleep due to the worry, and the situation became untenable. Jonathan decided he must move.

That alone was a major decision, for his family had farmed this land for generations, but Jonathan, in his misery, felt it was the only sensible course. He and his wife found some more premises and prepared for the move. He transferred most of his belongings and the livestock without any problem and was left with the final bits and pieces. He loaded these onto a cart and began his final journey.

A friend, who had been away and had not heard of their troubles, saw the cart approaching and waved it to a halt.

'Noo then, Jonathan, what's gahin on?' he asked.

Jonathan explained his troubles and added, 'So, you see, we're flitting.'

And to his horror, the lid of a milk churn was raised and a small, brown and wizened face peered out.

'Aye,' said the hob. 'We're flitting.'

This story is widely repeated, even overseas and there is a Danish and Norwegian equivalent involving an elf called a 'nisse'. No Scandinavian farm could ever succeed without the aid of a 'nisse' ... and in Scotland there was the 'Brownie'; in Germany the 'Kobold'; in Sweden the 'tomtgubbe'; in Holland, the 'redcap' and in other parts of Britain, there was 'Puck'. In other countries, there are similar imps and elves, but in Farndale the hob reigned supreme. See the Glaisdale chapter, for other hob stories.

6   Freeborough Hill

The sleeping knights of Freeborough

Freeborough Hill is a conical mound rising to a shade over 800 feet in height. It lies a short distance within the new county of Cleveland, having previously been situated in the North Riding of Yorkshire. In spite of a change in its parent county, however, Freeborough Hill remains within the North York Moors National Park and it is about a mile south of Moorsholm. It stands close to the A171 Guisborough-to-Whitby road some five miles from Guisborough and is not far from Robin Hood's Butts where, it is said, during his many visits to this area, the hero from Sherwood Forest came to practise his archery.

Freeborough lies between two popular reservoirs – Scaling Dam and Lockwood Beck. Scaling Reservoir is the largest area of inland water within the North York Moors and it is rich with wildlife. With a picnic area and car-park, it is a popular venue for watersports, fishing and the observance of wildlife, Lockwood Beck is quieter, being favoured by anglers and wildlife observers. There is no watersport here, although fishing by boat is allowed and boats can be hired. A 'Trust the Angler' scheme is operated at Lockwood Beck where fishing permits may be obtained from late March until October.

The curious shape of Freeborough Hill has, over the centuries, resulted in a continuing mystique and there are many stories or rumours about it. One story suggests there is a deep pit shaft running directly from the summit

43

into the depths of the earth, and that this was used to bury hundreds of dead soldiers and horses after bygone battles.

Some say it contains the bodies of those who died during the Black Death; indeed, a grave was found on the side of the hill during the last century. This was made of whinstone blocks, however, which had been carried three or four miles to this site, thus indicating a grave of some importance.

One of the continuing arguments is whether Freeborough Hill is a natural feature or whether it is man-made. It is almost certainly a natural mound, probably a relic of the Ice Age and one of several conical hills around the Moors, such as Roseberry Topping (see chapter twenty) or Blakey Topping (see chapter fourteen). It is probable that the Anglican Courts or 'Freeburghs' assembled here and another possibility is that the name of the hill may come from Freya, the goddess of fertility, or it could come from 'frithborn', the peace-bond or frankpledge of the Angles.

One powerful legend associated with Freeborough Hill is that deep inside the hill lies King Arthur surrounded by the twelve knights of the Round Table. They are all asleep and waiting until they are once again required to save England from tyranny.

In the days of King Edward II (1284-1327), there was a farmer called Edward Trotter who lived in a small holding in Dimmingdale, not far from the slopes of Freeborough Hill. Edward hailed from the Skelton district and came to work this farm in the middle of Moorsholm Moor, bringing with him his wife and three children. He was a diligent farmer and worked his land well, and he was content with his quiet but busy life.

One evening in May, as the sun was setting, Edward was on the lower slopes of Freeborough, counting his sheep to see if any had been attacked by the wolves which roamed the lonely moors. He was making sure all the lambs and their mothers were safe when a ewe and her lamb ran off, apparently frightened by something Edward could not see, and he followed. They vanished around the side of Freeborough Hill and he was in time to see the ewe disappear into a large hole, rather like a badger sett or a large rabbit warren. The lamb followed. Thick briars grew around the hole and some of the sheep's wool got caught as she hurried into the tunnel. He arrived at the entrance, panting after the effort, but saw no sign of his sheep and lamb. He called, knowing it was useless for sheep are silly beasts; there was no response and he did not have a trained dog to send into the tunnel to find them. He did have a lantern, however, to light his way home should darkness fall before he finished work, and he used it as he ventured into the tunnel. Once inside, it was large enough to crawl comfortably along, but as he moved deeper inside the hill, the tunnel grew larger with each passing step.

Soon, Edward could walk upright and as he went deeper and deeper, he realized that, in the distance, there was a strange grey light. It was shining through a gap at the far end of the passage. Now he was walking briskly, thinking the grey light meant that the tunnel opened into the countryside at the other side of Freeborough Hill and that his sheep and her lamb had reached safety in the vanishing daylight beyond: but he was wrong. As Edward hurried nearer to the strange light, he saw that he was not approaching an exit but, instead, was walking towards a huge underground chamber which was bathed in this curious glow. As he moved nearer, cautious but not afraid, he realized that a door lay between him and the chamber. The door was partly open. It was sufficiently open to allow the light to reach him. Made of heavy oak, it was studded with metal and the large iron handle was smothered in cobwebs. He touched it lightly, and it swung open to its fullest extent with the slightest of creaks as Edward stepped into the chamber. As he entered, he kicked a metal goblet which lay on the floor; it clanked slightly against a stone and then Edward experienced a terrible shock.

Standing behind the door, on guard, was a man in chain mail. He was bearing a long spear in one hand and a sword in the other. As Edward realized the man was there, the man seemed to awake from a deep, deep sleep; at the same time, as the echoes of the kicked goblet sounded around the chamber, so there came the sounds of other men rousing and groaning ...

Edward turned to run, but the spear halted him.

'Stay,' ordered the guard.

'Who are you?' asked Edward.

'Hush!' commanded the guard, who pointed his spear into the centre chamber. Edward could see more men in similar dress; they were seated around a large circular table, but their heads rested on the table in the deepest of sleeps. Goblets and plates were scattered around and all had swords dangling from their belts. And then, glinting in the curious dim grey light, Edward saw a crown. It glittered with gold and precious stones, and was lying on the table beside a man who was larger than the others. But he too was fast asleep.

'You almost aroused them,' said the guard in a faint whisper. 'Who are you, pray?'

'I am Edward Trotter the farmer,' said Edward. 'I am seeking a lost sheep and her lamb.'

'They are not here, as you can see,' the guard allowed Edward a few moments to peer around the chamber. There were no other doors and nowhere for his sheep to hide. In those few moments, Edward could not help noticing the greyness of the sleeping knights and their king, the musty smell that pervaded, the cobwebs that smothered almost everything in the room ...

'Who are they?' asked Edward of the guard.

'We are King Arthur and his Knights of the Round Table,' he was told. 'We are sleeping until our services are again required to free England from tyranny. Now, you must go, you have seen more than any other man alive. You must tell no one of what you have seen, no one. Is that understood?'

'Yes, of course, I mean, no, I will tell no one ...'

'Then go, Edward Trotter, before it is too late.'

With a quick last look at the still sleeping noblemen, Edward hurried from the chamber and the door closed behind him with a solid thud. Suddenly, it was dark for the grey light from the chamber had now been cut off. The meagre light of his lantern was barely sufficient to find his way along the passage which grew narrower and lower with every step he took. Now terrified, he ran as fast as he could, then crawled the final yards, welcoming the scent of the fresh evening air which now filtered into the passage and suddenly he was outside again. He found himself standing close to the briars on the slopes of Freeborough Hill at the exact place the sheep had entered earlier. The sheep and her lamb were there, grazing on the hillside as if nothing had happened.

Edward went home in a daze and in bed that night, he could not sleep. His wife asked what was the matter, why he had been so long in returning from his sheep count, and what was on his mind? At length, he told her, momentarily forgetting the sentry's warning.

'You must show me the chamber in the morning,' she said.

'And you must not tell anyone of what you see,' he told her for now he remembered the sentry's warning. 'I was told not to tell anyone, no one at all. Promise me you will not tell anyone, not even the children.'

'I promise,' said his wife, and both sank into a deep and refreshing sleep.

But the next morning, when he took his wife to the place where the sheep had vanished, there was no sign of the entrance to the knights' chamber. The briars were there, but there was no tunnel, not even a rabbit warren. And when he pressed a stick into the earth, it was solid.

'But ...' he tried to explain to his wife.

'I think you fell asleep here last night,' she smiled. 'Your lost sheep are safe; I think you dreamt the whole thing.'

But ever since that day, no one has been able to find that entrance to the chamber of the knights on the side of Freeborough Hill. Meanwhile, deep inside the curious mound, King Arthur and his Knights of the Round Table slumber on until England requires them.

7 Fryup

Fairy Cross Plain

Fryup consists of two dales, the larger known as Great Fryup Dale and the lesser as Little Fryup Dale. Each has a beck, the local name for a moorland stream, and these are, not surprisingly, known as Great Fryup Beck and Little Fryup Beck. Both are tributaries of the River Esk and they enter that river between Danby and Lealholm. There is no village in Fryup, for the community comprises a number of scattered farms and moorland cottages in spectacular surroundings.

Each of the Fryup dales extends south-west from Eskdale, pushing into the centre of the moors like twin fingers of lush greenery in a sea of surrounding heather and expansive wilderness. Danby Castle stands near the entrance to Little Fryup Dale, while the curiously named Fryup Street forms part of the route around the valley. This is a steep, narrow hill between a few scattered dwellings. Along the south-west corner of Little Fryup Dale is Crossley Sides, a stretch of moorland known for its delicious wild bilberries which add a touch of moorland air to home-made pies and puddings. Another curiosity, high in the dale head of Great Fryup, was the George Gap Spa. This was a dangerous bog below the moor edge whose water was stained deep rust colour by the minerals it contained.

A hint of a long-dead industry in Fryup is contained in the name of Furnace Farm, for iron-ore was smelted here in days long past. The iron was carried out of Fryup by pack horses and taken into Whitby to be shipped to its customers. In 1271, some seven furnaces were operating in this area and mounds of cinders have provided fairly recent evidence of their presence.

Fryup's strange name causes speculation among residents and visitors alike, but it has nothing to do with the Yorkshire custom of having a huge fry-up for breakfast or any other meal as some writers have suggested. It is probably derived from 'Friga', an Old English personal name, while 'up' or 'hop' means a small valley. Around 1223, the dale was known as 'Frihop' and around a century later, it had changed to 'Frehoper', the pronunciation of which (especially in the dialect of the region) is very like the modern Fryup. The name may mean Friga's Valley.

The eastern road into Great Fryup Dale used to boast six gates within the first mile of its length, but eventually these were removed. A commemorative stone says, 'Six gates in next mile a nuisance proved. Helped by kind donors, tenants and others had them removed. USE WELL TIME SAVED.'

Fryup seems to like its inscriptions because the original school building, no longer used as such, bore a stone which read, 'THIS SCHOOL WAS ERECTED BY VOLUNTARY SUBSCRIPTION, AD MDCCCVIII. TRAIN UP A CHILD IN THE WAY HE SHOULD GO AND WHEN HE IS OLD HE WILL NOT DEPART FROM IT.'

Another inscription on the same school said, 'STRANGER, WHOEVER THOU ART, CAST IN THY LOT AMONG US. LET US HAVE BUT ONE PURSE. BLESSED ARE THE POOR FOR THE LORD WILL HAVE MERCY UPON THEM IN THE DAY OF TROUBLE', while yet another tablet said, 'THROUGH ALL THINGS, WHATSOEVER YE WOULD THAT MEN SHOULD DO UNTO YOU, DO YE ALSO EVEN UNTO THEM.' One of the subjects taught until 1850 in this remote inland school was navigation!

The twin dales of Fryup meet to the south of the elevated oval-shaped barrier which separates them. The southerly tip of that rising piece of moorland is called

Fairy Cross Plain, a name which dates to more than two centuries, and accordingly to local folklore, this used to be the haunt of fairies.

The 'cross' portion of its name is said to come from the moorland tracks which once met here. One of them went around the twin dales while the other went south via the steep slopes of Stainch Bullen to join the route which now forms a link between Danby Castle and Rosedale. This track linked Danby Castle with Pickering Castle, and was the route taken by Edward II when he journeyed from Pickering Castle to Whorlton Castle, staying overnight at Danby Castle *en route*. His journey took a whole week. Now it could be done within an hour.

The area of moorland around the concourse of these tracks was once rich with fairy rings. These were natural circles on the ground and they were created by fungi, one of which is known as Fairy Ring Champignon (*marasmius oreades*). This is edible and sometimes grows on domestic lawns.

The name of fairy ring fungus has been applied to other fungi, and the name of 'fairy ring' was sometimes given to circles of small white or yellow flowers which appeared in meadows.

Superstitious people of the past regarded them as magical in some way and tradition said that fairy rings were places where the fairies gathered to dance. Some thought they marked the location of an underground fairy village and if anyone ran around them nine times in the light of a full moon, they would be able to hear the fairies laughing and playing under the earth. It was not wise, however, to attempt this on nights such as the Eve of May Day or Hallowe'en for those nights were given entirely to the fairies. Trespassing upon their merrymaking could give rise to later problems.

In the case of the Fryup fairy rings, children would play around them while making sure they never ran more than nine times around any particular one. If they did, it was thought the fairies would acquire some kind of power over them or even whisk them away for ever into their fairy tunnels beneath the ground. It was said that sheep and cattle would never graze near these rings, recognizing the dangers they held, while the local people believed it was dangerous to attempt to remove such a ring. Things associated with the fairies were best left alone.

If we tend to scoff at such beliefs, it is the case that stories of the presence of fairies on Fairy Cross Plain were strong even at the beginning of this century. Canon J.C. Atkinson in his *Forty Years on a Moorland Parish* (1908) records such an account at this very place. In the dialect of the dale, the fairies were said to have 'a desper't haunt o' thae hill ends'. At the time, there was an inn near Fairy Cross Plain, and it was said that the fairy rings behind the inn were the largest and most regular of any in the district.

Canon Atkinson spoke to one man who, when a child, had been told by his mother that if he misbehaved he would be turned out of doors at night so that the fairies could take him away for ever. And as a child about a century ago, he believed it.

One old lady of the dale gives a graphic account of sighting of fairies here. It is in the dialect of the time and when asked if she had ever seen the fairies, she said, 'Aye, many a tahm and offens. They used to come down t'hill by this deear (door) and gaed in at yon brig-steean.' She meant they would come down the hill near her door, and then go in (underground) at the stone which supported the bridge where there was a culvert. She then went on to describe one fairy as a little green man wearing a queer sort of a cap. As she was rendering this account to Canon Atkinson, her disbelieving husband interrupted by saying, 'Where do they live then?'

'Under the ground, to be sure,' she retorted.

'Nay, nay,' said the husband. 'How can they live under t'grund?'

'Why t'mouldiwarps does, so why can't fairies?' snapped the lady. Mouldiwarps are moles.

The lady went on to say that she had heard the fairies at night, busying themselves with sounds like butter-making. One of their night-time activities was thought to be the manufacture of fairy-butter. She showed Canon Atkinson a gate near which she had heard the fairies at work 'as plain as plain, and in the morning, the butter was clamed (smeared) all over t'main part o' t'gate'.

She then went on to describe the discovery of a fairy-bairn (a child fairy). A local lass had found it while hay-making; as she had raked over the dried hay, she had uncovered the fairy child and these are the old lady's words, with standard English ones added to clarify the tale:

> It was liggin' [lying] in a swathe of the half-made hay, as bonny as lahtle [little] thing as ever yan seen. But it was a fairy-bairn, it was quite good to tell. But it did not stay lang [long] wi' t'lass that fun [found] it. It sooart o' dwinied [withered] away and she aimed [supposed] the fairy-mother couldn't deea [do] wivoot it any langer [longer].

It seems that the old lady in question was something of a story teller, for she told of a troll living on the hill behind Fairy Cross Plain, and of dwarfs living near the coast.

She was passing along the folk tales of many centuries in a manner which implied her implicit belief in them, and one of her stories is that of the Hart Hall Hob which appears in chapter eight.

And are there still fairies in Fryup? If you care to visit Fairy Cross Plain at midnight on Hallowe'en when there is a full moon, you might just hear them laughing and playing beneath those fairy circles ...

8 Glaisdale

The hob of Hart Hall, and a witch!

There is little doubt that Glaisdale is a major centre of folklore within the North York Moors. Situated deep in the Esk Valley nine miles or so from Whitby, it boasts a remarkable and graceful seventeenth century bridge which is a reminder of a romance associated with the Spanish Armada (see chapter one); there is a farm which was home of a hob; a tale of a witch hare which troubled the folk of the dale head; the story of a stunning leap by a hunted deer; a wishing stone set deep in a local wood; a Lover's Leap; a Dead Man's Pool and even a cave which was used as a hideaway by Robin Hood, complete with a secret tunnel leading to Robin Hood's Bay.

In an old guide, the village was described as having many natural charms, for it is among meandering streams and wooded vales. All around are the beautiful moors and, indeed, Arthur Mee, in his *King's England* series, said it was cut off from the world by the moors. Today, it is a straggling village with its rows of dark stone cottages set on dramatic hillsides. There are three inns, a parish church and a dale stretching three miles into the depths of the moors where there was once a thriving weaving industry. The village school occupies a stunning position on the edge of open moorland while the music of the skylark and curlew can be heard all around the district.

During the last century, Glaisdale was a vital source of iron-ore which helped to establish Middlesbrough as a major steel-producing town. Blast furnaces operated between 1866 and 1876 but few scars remain. One reminder, however, is the route of a railway line which was to take the iron-ore from Glaisdale across the moors to Skinningrove Iron Works. Work began in 1873 with sidings, cuttings and even bridges being completed; indeed, the Railway Hotel was built at Moorsholm, but the line never opened. It suffered a series of mishaps and only its path across the moors can be seen – as children, we called it the Paddy Waddle Railway in memory of Mr John Waddell and his team of Irish labourers who planned to build it.

I was born and brought up in Glaisdale, living there until my early twenties, and so these folk stories were part of my life. They were passed from generation to generation by word of mouth in the traditional manner, and several were given authenticity by surviving evidence.

I will start with Arncliffe Wood which offers a delightful walk from Glaisdale Railway Station to The Delves at Egton Bridge. As a child, that wood was my playground. It was here that I spent many happy hours and where I sought the cave of Robin Hood. Relying on information supplied by word of mouth, I calculated that it was midway through the wood overlooking the River Esk. This meant extensive exploration and I did find a mysterious rock shaped like a tank and bearing the initials J.A.R.

I also found the remains of a long-gone footbridge which had once crossed the tumbling river, I found Lover's Leap, a cliff overlooking the river from which two lovers leapt to their deaths long ago. Now it presides over an iron railway bridge which crosses the Esk below. Nearby is Dead Man's Pool where an unknown man drowned in years gone by and whose ghost was said to haunt the woodland. I found the wishing stone, a huge square rock with a tree growing through the centre, and many is the time I have climbed upon that rock to walk nine times round the tree while making a wish. The rock is still there but the tree is dead and as a child, I would find pennies tucked away in crevices, evidence of the continuing belief in the magic power of that rock. Even in the first half of this century, some people still paid the mysterious spirit of the wishing stone in the hope that their dreams would materialize.

But I never found Robin Hood's Cave. I knew it was large enough to accommodate Robin and his Merry Men, and I was told there were steps leading down to it because the floor was below ground level and covered with layers of beech leaves. It was warm and dry inside, and leading from it was a long, underground passage which emerged at Robin Hood's Bay, ten miles directly to the east of Glaisdale. Most of us dismissed the tunnel as pure legend, but surely there was such a cave among those beech trees, even if it had never sheltered Robin Hood? But I have never found it.

Another of my schoolboy pleasures in the 1940s was to visit Hart Hall Farm which stands below the school at Glaisdale. My friend and I would sit and chat beside the flickering fire in the farm kitchen. It was an old fashioned iron range and the floor was of stone. The lighting was by oil lamps and on a dark autumn night the wind would howl around the buildings as the cattle, snug in their own accommodation near the house, would fidget in their stalls and rattle their securing chains. Crickets sometimes chirped in the hearth and the calm quality of life was like stepping back a century.

This farm has a wonderful atmosphere and is the focus of a marvellous folk tale, for it was the haunt of one of North Yorkshire's many hobs. These, perhaps under other names such as hobgoblins, elves, redcaps, leprechauns, pixies, brownies and so on, feature in the folklore of many countries, but on the North York Moors they are depicted as solitary, dwarf-like men who live with a particular family, usually on a farm, and there undertake various odd jobs. They are often described as shaggy-haired and ugly, and many of them work naked, detesting clothes to such an extent that they become annoyed if offered any. They prefer to work and live away from prying eyes, but operate very swiftly and effectively, at times showing super-human strength and speed of operation.

One of their conditions is that they seek no reward for their work, other than perhaps a jug of cream or some other occasional token of gratitude.

There are many links with hobs around the moors, often in the name of locations and farms, such as Hob Cross, Hob Hill, Hob Green, Hob Thrush Grange, Hob Thrush Hall, Hob Dale, Hob Holes, Hob Moor, Hob Garth, Hob's Cave and so forth. There are many such names around the North York Moors and of the hobs named as living in and around the moors, there are Cross Hob of Lastingham, Elphi of Low Farndale, Hodge Hob of Barnsdale, Hob of Hasty Bank in Bilsdale, Dale Town Hob of Hawnby, the Hob of Chop Gate, the Goathland Hob of Howl Moor, Hob of Egton High Moor and the Scugdale Hob.

At Hart Hall Farm, Glaisdale, however, there lived a hob who was known far and wide. He was a kindly fellow, not at all mischievous like some and he always performed good deeds which were of immense value. He preferred to work around midnight but always in secret and he seemed to know what work was urgent and where best to address his skills.

One story concerns a loaded hay waggon whose wheel had become lodged between two stones on its way from the fields. The weather was threatening, with heavy rain likely to put the hay at risk, so it was vital that the hay, dried and neatly arranged hay cocks, was brought rapidly in from the fields.

Everything was going well until that wheel became jammed. The wagon was loaded at the time and extra horses and men could not free it. The matter was becoming urgent and it was necessary to unload the cart if it was to be freed, but this, and the re-loading was a time-consuming task.

As they discussed their problem, darkness descended. There was no way they could work with the available lighting and so they had to abandon the loaded cart and pray that no rain came during the night hours. Exhausted by their efforts, the tired workers fell into bed, determined to resume at dawn. But when everyone was asleep, the Hart Hall Hob started work. With his superior strength, he released the wheel and then drew the cart into the yard where he unloaded it, even stacking the hay. Then he prepared the cart for the next morning.

This was one example of his kind-hearted work. He also helped with the thrashing, ploughing, sowing, harrowing, stacking and all the routine work of the farm. He was always available when needed and never had to be asked for assistance. In this case, there is an account of the Hart Hall Hob actually seen at work. It was a moonlit night in the autumn when a farm lad chanced to hear the hob working in a barn. He was threshing with a flail, and the lad could hear the distinctive and rhythmic beat of the swipple. He peered through a small hole in the door and saw a little brown man, all covered with hair, skilfully threshing by hand.

He had a pile of sheafs on the floor and rapidly reduced them to straw and corn. He wore no clothes, except for a very ragged and rough working shirt known as a sark. When this lad told the others, they decided to make him a new sark with which to wrap himself (summat ti hap hisself wiv) and so produced a hessian working shirt with a belt around the middle.

When it was finished, they took it to the barn and laid it out, ready for his next visit. It never occurred to them that they might be insulting the hob, or that he might object on the grounds they had been spying on him while at work. But they all watched him in secret as he picked up the sark and examined it. Now, he realized he was being watched, but he was a sweet-tempered hob and turned to face his benefactors, explaining that he always worked naked and must never accept a gift. These were his words,

'Gin hob mun hae nowt but a harding hamp
He'll cum nae mair, nowther to berry nor stamp.'

'Harding' means hessian, while a 'hamp' was a rough

working shirt; 'berry' means to thresh and 'stamp' means to knock off the beards of barley prior to threshing it.

Having said that, the hob left Hart Hall and was never seen again.

There is a wonderful account of this incident in the dialect of the moors. It comes from an old lady and I repeat part of it here:

> Yah moonleeght neeght, when they heeard his swipple gannan wiv a strange quick bat on t'lathe fleear (ye ken he wad deea mair i' yah neeght than a' t'men o' t'farm iv a deea), yan o' t'lads gat hissel croppen oop close anenst t'lathe-deear, an' leeaked in thruff a lahtle hole i' t'booards, an' he seen a lahtle brown man, a' covered wi' hair, spanging aboot wiv t'fleeal lahk yan wad.
>
> He'd getten a haill dess o' shaffs doon on t'fleear and My Wod! Ommost afore ye could tell ten, he had tonned out t'strae, an' sided away t'coorn, and was rife for another dess. He had neea cleeathes on ti speak of and t'lad, he could see 'at he had neea mak or mander o' duds bar an aud ragged soort o' sark …

While Hart Hall lies towards the bottom or 'end' of Glaisdale dale, there is another folk story associated with the 'head' or top of the dale, around Hob Intake near Hob Garth. This concerns a witch-hare: a woman thought capable of turning herself into a hare. There were many of these ladies around the moors – Jane Grear from Guisborough who was bitten by a dog while galloping in the form of a hare, Peggy Flaunders of Marske-by-the-Sea who was hunted as a hare and bitten on the haunch, Jane Wood who lived in Baysdale, Nan Hardwicke who lived near Danby (see chapter five), Nanny Pearson of Goathland and Peg Humphrey of East Moor near Helmsley who was reputedly shot while in the form of a hare. She was nothing more than a harmless woman. Her story is told in my *Portrait of the North York Moors* as by Nicholas Rhea.

This is the account of the Glaisdale witch-hare. A farmer at the dale head became aware of 'no mere ordinary hare', it was biting the tops off some young saplings and he decided to lay in wait and shoot it. Knowing it might be a witch-hare, he loaded his gun with silver shot fashioned from old silver buttons, then concealed himself near his nursery.

At midnight, the hare appeared and began nipping off the buds whereupon the farmer raised his gun and opened fire. The barrage of silver pellets hit the hare and it shrieked horribly then tried to run out of the nursery towards a house known to be occupied by Awd Maggie, the reputed witch. Around the house was an area of scrubland known for a long time afterwards as Witch Hill and the hare fled into that, and then vanished. Next day, Maggie was discovered lying in bed with wounds to her thigh and back; she explained this by saying she had fallen on some broken glass. The hare was never found alive or dead.

Evidence of yet another story of an animal can be found on Glaisdale Rigg which is upon the moors overlooking Witch Hill and Hob Intake. At a point close to where no less than eight moorland tracks converge, there is a point still known as Hart Leap (which has no links with Hart Hall further down the dale). It is marked by two stones which stand more than forty feet apart and one of them is inscribed with the words 'Hart's Leap'.

The story is that a huge hart was being pursued by deer-hounds and hunters and it had evaded them all day. But as the hart fled across the moors between Fryup and Glaisdale, it knew that capture was inevitable. It had to make one desperate attempt to avoid the hounds for they were now gaining fast, and at the point where those eight tracks met, the deer made a prodigious leap. As the ground was soft, it left imprints of its hoots in the earth, both where it began its leap and where it landed.

The hunters were so astonished at this massive leap that they decided to mark the place with two large stones and engraved them clearly so that the efforts of that unfortunate hart would be known for ever. The legend does not tell us the fate of the deer, however.

Whether it was allowed to escape or whether it suffered the fate of so many others during a hunt, we do not know.

9   Goathland

The Gytrash of Goathland

In its moorland setting, Goathland is one of North Yorkshire's most picturesque and interesting villages. It nestles in a hollow among the heather and is some 500 feet above sea level, just off the Whitby-Pickering moor road (A169). In the shadow of Fylingdales Ballistic Missile Early Warning Station, it boasts fine houses, quality hotels and interesting shops. It lies on the route of the North York Moors Steam Railway which has a station here.

Before the Steam Railway revived this beautiful stretch of track, it belonged to British Rail who closed the line. But long before nationalization, there was a fascinating railway from Grosmont to Pickering via Goathland. It has a renowned history – it was only the third railway line to be built in England where George Stephenson helped with the work. The original coaches were horse-drawn up the gradient between Beck Hole and Goathland and the incline was so steep that coaches were hauled up by a rope and a revolving drum. The weight was balanced by a huge water tank weighing four tons: it descended as the coaches ascended. Dickens travelled this line and described it as 'a quaint old railway'. Today, the line is busy again in its private role, linking with British Rail at Grosmont.

The village centre has wide grass verges which are shorn smooth by wandering moorland sheep and visitors can be startled by these animals for they are tame enough to attempt to take titbits. Some will even try to enter cars in their pursuit of food, but the owners of the animals do not like them being fed in this way – some of the offerings are both dangerous and bad for the sheep.

Goathland is an excellent central point for exploration of the moors and coastline, as well as being rich with interest in its own right. Several delightful waterfalls, known locally as fosses, are within walking distance, including the beautiful Mallyan Spout, seventy-feet-high waterfall which is gained via a footpath leading behind the Mallyan Spout Hotel. Nelly Ayre Foss is a short distance upstream and Thomasson Foss is downstream on the Murk Esk.

Goathland is the home of a sword-dance team known as the Goathland Plough Stots whose displays in the district are thought to have Viking origins of more than 1,000 years ago. The word 'stot' means a bullock, and it was the name given to the young men who towed a plough around the village on Plough Monday as they sang and danced while raising money for the church and local charities. Today's Plough Stots are really an amalgamation of those lads and a local sword-dancing team, one of several which practised and competed against one another in this area.

There is a great deal of ancient history around Goathland. Flints, axe heads and burial mounds on the surrounding moors, plus an ancient village now known as the Killing Pits, are evidence of ancient civilizations, while the nearby Roman road, one and a quarter miles in length, reveals the Roman influence on the district (see Wade's Causeway, chapter twenty-nine). On Fylingdales Moors are more than 1,000 cairns covering a square mile and they may be associated with an ancient burial ground. In the twelfth century, Henry I granted some land in Goathland for a hospital to be built plus 'a caracute of land for Osmund the priest'. Thus was St Mary's Hermitage established in 1117, and the present church, built in 1894-6, is dedicated to St Mary. Among the relics from earlier buildings on the site are a font, a seventeenth-century pulpit and a huge altar stone thought to have come from the hermitage. A silver chalice dated 1450 is believed be one of only two of its type in the country.

One of the fascinations of Goathland is its name. There had never been a Lord of the Manor, and many believe the name comes from goats (a strange goat folk story follows) but it probably relates to Goda, a Scandinavian settler or the Swedish Goths. It could even come from 'Gode Land' meaning God's Land, a name given by early Christian settlers, probably Normans. It seems that the hermitage was the first real community here. Down the years, the name has been spelt 'Godeland', 'Golanda', 'Gotheland', 'Goodland', 'Gotland', 'Goteland' and even 'Goutland' until the modern form was adopted.

There are sporting links with Goathland too. For many years it was a focal point for the hunting of deer and wild boar, and the men of Goathland were charged in 1612, by James I, with looking after the peregrine falcons kept for hawking by the King at Killingnoble Scar near Levisham. Foxhunting became fashionable with the founding, in 1750, of the Goathland Hunt. One of their whips, Tom Ventress, lived to be 101 and died in 1922, England's oldest huntsman.

Among all the legends and folklore surrounding Goathland, surely the story of the Gytrash is outstanding for its horror and menace. The story centres upon a castle built on a site still known as Julian Park. It is now a farmhouse on the road from Goathland to Egton Bridge and is about two miles from Goathland. It is on the route of a Roman road which crossed Wheeldale Moor and passed here on its way to Grosmont, and some theories are that the name is in honour of Julius Caesar whose men may have constructed a station here. Another theory is that the name comes from St Julian who was patron saint of travellers, innkeepers and hospitallers. Many religious establishments with a nursing role bore his name, so perhaps this is the site of Goathland's original hermitage/hospital?

In later years, it became known as July Park and was the site of a small community, but it was also the location of a castle built by the de Mauleys, a local landowning family. Now, it is called Julian Park; when the land surrounding the building ceased to be a park is not known.

Julian de Mauley built the castle which still bears his name. The date is uncertain, but it would probably be long before the Norman conquest, even dating to the time of King Arthur and his Knights of the Round Table. The castle would have been a small and rather primitive structure but at that time it was believed that if a living creature was incarcerated within the walls or beneath the foundations of a new building, then the structure would survive for centuries. Primitive pagan beliefs said that if a virgin was walled up, then that ensured even greater security. As this belief persisted in Julian de Mauley, he decided to incarcerate the loveliest of the local maidens within the walls of his new castle.

He selected the daughter of a mill-owner called Gudrun; she was called Gytha and was the most beautiful of the maidens in this area, the one desired by most of the young men. Julian gave orders for the girl to be seized and brought to Julian Park. His actions caused a storm of protest among the people of Goathland, but he refused to back down: he wanted to show them that he was the master of Julian Park. Gudrun was brave enough to face the evil man in a vain attempt to save his daughter from an awful, lingering death, but Julian would listen to no one. He even said that Gudrun would be the man to construct the walls around his daughter and when Gudrun refused, he was taken away and tortured by Julian's men.

Eventually, he lost the strength and will-power to refuse and so, as the new castle was built, Gudrun found himself having to construct that part of its wall which would seal in his daughter forever. Eventually, with Gytha weeping in her sorrow, there were only two stones left to be fixed in position. Someone gave Gytha a tumbler of water and some bread, and then Julian gave her a spinning wheel and lots of yarn to while away the dreadful period until her agonizing death. In a moment of awful cruelty, he said she must be kept busy even in her final moments. Finally the last stones were put in place and sealed. Gytha was entombed in what was to become her grave.

Many of the local people pleaded with Julian for the girl's release, but he steadfastly refused. Even the local holy men and priests made their pleas, but Julian would heed none. For many nights afterwards, she could be heard weeping in her dreadful misery but no one could release her. And so Gytha paid with her life.

Exactly one year later, Julian was contemplating some extensions to his castle. It was late in the evening and he was lying in his bed as he went over the plans in his mind. But as he lay, there came a terrible wailing noise which grew closer by the minute and Julian found he was immobilized. He could move neither hands nor feet and then the door of his room opened with a crash. In floated a figure dressed in the very gown that Gytha had worn when entombed in his castle wall.

The figure also carried the spindle of a spinning wheel. Without a word, she came to stand at the foot of his bed, looking down upon the terrified man in a awesome silence and menace. And then, as if wrapping him in an invisible thread, she moved the spindle over the foot of his bed, binding his feet and ankles so that they felt cold and dead. With that, the figure vanished and the wailing ceased. She vanished as suddenly as she had arrived. But when he tried to move, he found his feet were paralysed; he could only hobble around with the aid of a stick but he could see no threads.

On the anniversary of that night, the figure reappeared and wound more invisible thread around Julian's legs, making them dead from below the knees and this continued for ten more years. In that time, the figure wrapped more of her thread around Julian each year until more and more of his body was paralysed. He asked for holy men to pray for him, he said he would become a Christian and build a church, and said he would do good for the community and the people of Goathland forever, but nothing worked. The apparition continued to visit Julian de Mauley until he was completely paralysed until one night, during a massive storm, he died.

It was on that night that the terrible Gytrash appeared for the first time. It was said to be the spirit of the dead Julian. It had the features of a huge, black goat whose eyes blazed red, like a fire coal, and its horns were also tipped with fire.

The appearance of the Gytrash brought chaos and fear to the village. If anyone was unfortunate enough to be on the highways when the Gytrash appeared, it would follow them and chase them as they ran faster and faster. If it managed to overtake that person, the person would then die. In death, therefore, Julian was terrifying the people as he had done in those early days at Julian Park.

Goathland now had two spirits because the mysterious girl and her spindle of invisible thread was still operating on the anniversary of Gytha's death. But instead of turning her attention to Julian, she was selecting the fairest maids of the district and binding them with her thread. They began to die in horror and every midnight, on the anniversary of her death, a dreadful wailing could be heard from within the walls of Julian Park. The people asked their holy men and priests to exorcize these evil spirits, but nothing worked. The two evil spirits continued to terrify the people of Goathland until someone sought advice from the Spaewife of Fylingdales. She was a witch and was thought to be the best in the area, but her response was to utter these words, 'Tane to tither'. No one knew what she meant and she would not elaborate. For several weeks, the elders puzzled over her words until someone realized what the Spaewife meant. 'What she means is this,' said the wise man, 'You make one spirit deal with the other!'

Now they realized that the magic threads of the ghostly maiden could be used to bind the Gytrash, for surely the two spirits were sworn enemies? The problem was how to persuade them to appear together and so they returned to the Spaewife for more advice. She reminded them that Gytrashes have a liking for freshly buried corpses because that is from where they draw life, and so they would have to arrange a fake funeral. They should arrange the funeral to take place at the Killing Pits. But how could they persuade the spinning maid to go there too? 'Never fear,' said the Spaewife. 'She is the sworn enemy of the Gytrash, she will find him. All you must do is to mark with honey the trail from Julian Park to the Killing Pits, and then sprinkle it with corn and salt. She will follow.'

And so the people made a fake dead baby from a mell baby (a doll used for the celebrations of cutting the last sheaf of corn). They dressed the mell baby in some burial clothes and placed it in a coffin; the coffin was then carried, before midnight, to a new grave at the Killing Pits. It was lowered into the grave with all the ceremonial of a proper funeral and the people retreated to a distance to await the forthcoming battle.

At midnight precisely, the white-clad maid, with a spindle in her hand, materialized from the walls of the castle at Julian Park. In the meantime, the Gytrash had also appeared at the graveside and it descended into the new grave to start opening the coffin.

At this stage, the spirit of Gytha moved swiftly across the moors and stood beside the grave, there to wind her invisible threads around the Gytrash as it was in the grave. It issued the most terrible cries of anguish as she continued to bind it with threads and then the side of the grave collapsed and covered the Gytrash. It was now buried and unable to scramble out because it was immobilized by the threads.

Having achieved this, the ghost of Gytha dropped her spindle on the moors and vanished from sight.

Neither of these spirits has been active since that time, more than a thousand years ago, but there is still a strange feeling of mystery around the Killing Pits and the whole of the Goathland moors.

10 Guisborough

The raven and the chest of gold

Guisborough, splendidly situated beneath the tree-covered northern edge of the North York Moors, is one of the fine market towns that enrich the area. It is an ancient place which has much to offer, and it makes an excellent centre for exploration of the moors, the dales and the coastline. There are thriving markets on Thursdays and Saturdays, and there is a great deal of history associated with the town and surrounding area.

It now lies within County Cleveland, but until 1974 was an important North Riding of Yorkshire trading centre. It continues to fulfil its trading role and draws people from the villages along the northern edge of the moors. It was once the capital of Cleveland, the name given to that part of the North York Moors which bordered the town and reached into the central parts of the moors. That area has now given its name to a new county which includes Guisborough, but which extends to cover Middlesbrough, Stockton, Thornaby and their satellite communities. Nonetheless, a large area of the former Cleveland district, including portions of the Cleveland Hills, are within the North York Moors National Park.

Guisborough has a wide and interesting main street with cafés, shops and inns, and within the town centre is an old market cross with a sundial.

The fifteenth-century church of St Nicholas is of great interest. It contains the unique Bruce Cenotaph which links the local de Brus (Bruce) family with King Robert the Bruce whose grandfather is buried at Guisborough Priory. The Cenotaph was saved from ruin during the Reformation when the priory was ransacked and dissolved, and it was placed in this church. It was presented to Guisborough Priory, probably by Margaret Tudor, the daughter of Henry VII and it depicts a remarkable chapter in the history of the famous Bruce families of both England and Scotland.

On the outskirts is Gisborough Hall, the seat of Lord Gisborough, each spelt without the 'u' which is in the name of the town. The Hall is noted for its collection of superb trees, especially a massive horse chestnut which was thought to date before the Dissolution of the priory; its branches sank to the ground and there took root to create a miniature wood in itself. Its trunk was twenty-three-feet in circumference.

The original Hall was built by Sir Thomas Challoner who was an ambassador to the Spanish Court. His son introduced alum mining to the Moors around 1595 but stole the secrets from no less a person than the Pope. He also persuaded many of the Pope's skilled alum workmen to leave Italy to work on the Moors and for that cheeky piece of business, he was excommunicated. These were the first alum mines in England.

Dominating the skyline at the east of the town, however, is the beautiful east window of the ruined priory which has a fifty-six-foot arch. These magnificent ruins are a short distance from the town centre and make a pleasing and peaceful excursion from the bustle of shops and traffic.

Permission to build the priory was given to Robert de Brus by Pope Calixtus II in 1119. The priory was for the Augustinian order of monks and was dedicated to The Blessed Virgin Mary. The first building was Norman in design and the second was English, but the latter burned down through the carelessness of a workman who was repairing the roof. He was melting lead to effect the repairs and went away for a break, leaving his fire blazing with disastrous consequences. The third church was built around 1309 and it was given 2,000 acres of land by another member of the de Brus family. At the Dissolution of the Monasteries, Guisborough was a very rich community, only Fountains, Selby and St Mary's in York being wealthier.

A local tale says that Guisborough Priory is haunted by the ghost of a Black Monk who returns once a year to inspect the ruins. He arrives at midnight at the first new moon of the year, and lets down a long-vanished drawbridge over an invisible moat.

But there is another folk story about these ruins and it lingers in the memories of many people, being oft repeated even into the early years of this century.

For many years, there had persisted a rumour that beneath the priory, even when it was a living community, there was a long underground passage. It began somewhere near that part of the priory which was closest to the town where one of its entrances could be found. It then descended beneath the bulk of the priory and emerged in open land about a mile and a half away. It seems that the presence of this tunnel was well known amongst the townspeople, but no one dared venture along it.

According to local folklore, mid-way along the tunnel there was a massive chest of gold which was guarded by a giant raven. If anyone tried to steal the gold, the raven would attack and drive them off, attempting to peck out their eyes. For that reason, none of the townspeople would explore the underground passage, nor did they even attempt to find either its entrance or its exit.

But one day, long before the priory was destroyed by Henry VIII's commissioners at the Dissolution, a man from Guisborough decided he would defy that raven and win the chest of gold. He was Crispin Tocketts, a cobbler of the town and a man well known for his individuality and daring. He knew of the reputed resting place of that gold and decided that no raven was large enough to deter him. He therefore sought the entrance and the exit, working out how long it would take to traverse the long tunnel and what kind of lights he must carry. He realized he may be under the ground for a long time, and that there might also be other tunnels leading from this one.

He therefore took with him a roll of sheep's wool. One end, he would fasten to a point at his entrance, then he would unroll it along the route so that he could retrace his steps if his lights expired. His lights comprised large candles and he also took a staff and a sword with which to protect himself.

A small amount of food completed his preparations and early one spring morning, Crispin began his journey. He decided to start at the end of the tunnel which was nearest the town, but had no idea whether it ran in a straight line or whether it twisted and curved beneath the ground. Tying his wool to a hawthorn bush near the entrance, he lit the first of his candles and descended the steep slope into the passage which marked the beginning of his adventure.

In the dim light of his candle, he made his way through the dark and narrow tunnel, sometimes treading in pools of water, sometimes frightening small mammals and bats, sometimes touching tree roots which had come through from the ground above and sometimes having to manoeuvre past falls from the roof and loose stones and sand. He found that the tunnel did twist and turn as it threaded its way beneath the priory, but fortunately, there were no other passages to confuse him.

His progress was slow. It was breathless down there and he had to stoop almost to his hands and knees in places, but Crispin never thought for one moment that he would fail. He simply plodded forward with dogged determination.

His gallant effort was rewarded for suddenly his dim light glinted from a huge chest which was standing on a plinth in a hollow carved from the earth. It was framed with large stones and rested on a strong stone table. Here was the treasure he sought! He ran towards it, his candle highlighting the stout wooden timbers, the iron bands around it, the clasp on the front and the brass plate which contained indecipherable lettering. But the legend was true!

Crispin placed his candle on the stone table beside the chest and tried to loosen the clasp – there was no lock, he noted – and in seconds, he was lifting the heavy lid. Inside, there was a mass of gold coins, silver coins, chalices and plates in gold and silver, a mitre in gold and silver with precious stones glittering around it.

But, at that moment, a huge black raven appeared. He heard its wing beats and felt the swish of air as it flew over his head and settled before him on the upraised lid. It glared at him, its weight pushing down the lid as he backed away. Then, as he released the lid so that it crashed back to its former position, the raven turned into the Devil.

And there before Crispin stood Satan himself, fiery and angry, domineering and terrifying and so Crispin ran. He forgot to bring his candle and fell over the wool which was his marker … in the darkness of that tunnel, Crispin Tocketts fled for his life.

He stumbled and crawled, he ran almost blind in the blackness, feeling his way along the dank walls as the sound of the Devil's voice roared in his wake.

When he finally stumbled, frightened, dirty and wet, into the fresh night air before the priory, he was a quivering wreck of a man and it was years before he could bring himself to tell anyone of his experience. But when the tale did circulate the town, it so frightened the people of Guisborough, that no one has since tried to find the hoard of gold which is guarded by that giant raven.

11 Hackness

The dream of Begu

There seems little to link the west coast Cumbrian village of St Bees with the fascinating and beautiful North Yorkshire moorland community of Hackness near Scarborough on the other side of England. More than a hundred miles separates these villages, but the connection is there and it dates to the seventh century. The link is a very holy nun known sometimes as 'St Bee' or more formally as 'St Bega' or 'St Begu'.

Little is known of this saint, except that her feast day is 31 October and that she was probably of Irish descent, being recruited to the church by St Aidan. Although we have little knowledge of her early life, we do know she was a member of a small monastery at Hackness.

Hackness is charming and full of interest. Lying deep in the valley of the River Derwent, it consists of lovely old cottages of local stone whilst a clear stream ripples beside the road near Hackness Hall, the home of Lord Derwent.

The village is surrounded by steeply wooded hills and lofty moors while the oddly named hamlets of Broxa and Silpho are on the heights. Nearby are some rocks known as Bridestones. Several valleys converge here, including the romantically named Whisperdales; one is so deep that it is said that it never receives any sunshine from October until March.

The Forestry Commission has planted vast numbers of conifers on the hills and there are some interesting walks and forest drives.

One famous son of Hackness is the sculptor, Matthew Noble who was born here. He carved London statues such as those of the Earl of Danby, Sir John Franklin and Sir James Outram, while he exhibited over 100 works at the Royal Academy. He is buried nearby at Brompton.

As befitting a village which once had a monastery, Hackness boasts an ancient and wonderful little church which, in its own early days, was also a Benedictine monastery. Thus Hackness has had two monasteries. William de Percy, who restored Whitby Abbey after the Norman Conquest, also owned the manor of Hackness, and his brother, Serlo, secured the right to build a Benedictine cell here around 1050. Serlo became its abbot and that cell is now the church.

It is dedicated to St Peter with some stones dating to the eighth century, although the present foundations were laid around 1050. It has a thirteenth-century tower topped by a fifteenth-century octagonal spire, a rarity in this part of England, while an arch to the nave is thought to date from Saxon times. Three bays leading to the north aisle date from 1200 and the stalls are over 400 years old, whilst the carved font and Jacobean pulpit are intriguing. The font has a magnificent tall oak cover carved in 1480, with eight figures in pearwood added later, having been carved in Oberammergau.

One rare item is an early Anglo-Saxon stone cross inscribed in Latin to the memory of Abbess Oethilburg who was in charge of the earlier Hackness monastery around AD 720; part of the inscription reads 'Blessed Oethilburg! For ever may they remember thee; dutifully mourning, may they ask for thy verdant rest in the name of Christ, venerable mother.' The monastery was founded in AD 680 by St Hilda of Whitby Abbey and was destroyed by the Danes in AD 869.

The reason for the founding of this first monastery at Hackness was that St Hilda or 'Hild' as she was then known, was ageing and required a peaceful cell to which she could retreat. She needed moments of solitude away from the hectic pace of running the busy abbey of Whitby. Then aged sixty-six, she had been in poor health for seven years and in AD 680, therefore, the year of her death in fact, she created the little cell at Hackness. The Venerable Bede writes, *'quod ipsa eodem anno construxerat, et appellatur Hacanos.'* We now call Hacanos 'Hackness'. It was some sixteen miles from Whitby and Hilda sent along some of the Whitby nuns to form the new, but small, community. One of them was Bega or 'Begu'. She had been a nun for thirty years and was a dependable woman, one in whom Hilda could place her trust for supervising the new cell during her absence.

Through Begu, we have an account of the ascension to heaven of a saint at the moment of death, surely a rare if not unique event. That saint was Hilda.

Perhaps the finest account of Begu's vision or dream is that told by the Venerable Bede himself. This is what he wrote about St Hilda's death:

In the seventh year of her sickness, being at Streanshalh*, her distemper turned inwards, and she came to her last day. About cock-crowing, having received the viaticum of the Holy Communion, she called together the servants of Christ that were within that monastery, admonishing them to preserve evangelical peace among themselves and with all others; and as she was yet making her speech, she joyfully met death, or, to speak in the words of Our Lord, passed from death to life.

That same night, it pleased the Almighty Lord, by a manifest vision, to make known her death in the monastery of Hakenes. For a certain nun there called Begu (who, having dedicated her virginity to God, had served him upwards of thirty years in monastical conversation) being then in the dormitory of the sisters, all of a sudden heard the sound of a bell in the air, which used to awake and call them to prayers, when any of them was taken out of this world. When opening her eyes, she saw, as she thought, the roof of the house laid open, and a glorious light coming in through the top of the

---

* Streanshalh – the old name for Whitby. This is just one of several ways of spelling the name.

same; at whose lustre being astonished, while she stedfastly looked thereon, she saw the soul of the aforesaid servant of God ascend to heaven in that same pillar of light, attended and conducted by angels.

After which awakening, and seeing the other sisters lying about her, she perceived that what she had seen was shewn her either in a dream or a vision: therefore, rising immediately, in a great fright, she ran to the virgin who then presided in that monastery in the Abbess's stead (her name being Frigyth) and shedding abundance of tears, she sighed, and told her, that their Abbess, the lady Hild, the Mother of them all, was departed out of this world, and had in her sight ascended to eternal bliss, and to the company of the heavenly citizens, surrounded with a glorious light and conducted by angels.

Frigyth, having heard this, awakened all the sisters and called them to the church, admonished them to pray and sing psalms for her soul; which they having done during the remaining part of the night, the brothers came in the morning by break of day, from the place where she deceased, with advice of her death.

The sisters answered they had known the same before: and then related how and when they heard it; by which it appeared that her death had been shewn to them in a vision at that very instant when the others said she had departed this world. Thus it was by heaven happily ordained, that when some saw her departure out of this world, others should be acquainted with her admittance into the eternal life of souls.

Those monasteries are about thirteen miles distant from each other. It is also reported that her death was made known in a vision to one of the virgins devoted to God, who loved her most passionately, and lived in the same monastery where this servant of God died. This nun saw the soul ascend into heaven with angels; and this she declared, the very hour it happened, to those servants of Christ that were with her; and awakened them to pray for her soul, even before the rest of the congregation had heard of her death.

The truth of this was known to the whole monastery in the morning; and the aforesaid nun was known at that time to be, with some other servants of Christ in the remotest part of the monastery, where the women newly come to conversion used to be upon trial, till such time as they were regularly instructed and admitted into the society of the congregation.

Thus died that most religious servant of Christ, Hild, Abbess of Streanshalh, after having performed many heavenly works. She passed from hence to receive the rewards to heavenly life, in the year of Our Lord's incarnation 680, on the 15th day of the kalends of December (the 17th of November) at the age of 66 years; the which she equally divided, spending the first thirty-three years by living most nobly and royally in a secular habit, and the other thirty-three she more nobly dedicated to Our Lord in a monastic life.

This account is of further interest because it contains what is believed to be the very first mention of a bell in ecclesiastical history (cf. *Whitby Lore and Legend* by Jeffrey Shaw, Horne, 1952). After witnessing this unique vision of a saint rising to heaven at the precise moment it occurred, Begu went back to Whitby (Streanshalh) Abbey where she remained for some time. Later, she was transferred to a small village on the west coast of Cumberland where she established another small monastery. That village and its monastery adopted her popular name, the name by which it is still known today – St Bees.

12 Handale

The serpent of Handale

Handale is a place of solitude about two miles south of Loftus. Until the boundary changes of 1974, this lay within the North Riding of Yorkshire but it is now part of Cleveland county. However, Handale retains its Yorkshire links due to its position precisely upon the northern boundary line of the North York Moors National Park.

Its remoteness makes it ideal for the establishment of a monastery. It is located at the head of Grenedale or 'Grindale', as the tree-lined valley was once known. These names have long fallen into disuse, although it is thought that Grindale is preserved in the modern name of Grinkle which is nearby. Old records show names like 'Gryndale', 'Grindell' and 'Grenedale', with 'Handale' or 'Little Handales', once called 'Litlehandailes', being superimposed. 'Grenedale' perhaps suggests a green valley which is most apt.

A small stream flows through Handale; it rises on Waupley Moor and flows through a picturesque ravine towards Loftus, after which it becomes a tributary of Kilton Beck. Handale can be approached either by a footpath from the road near Grinkle Park or by a track from the minor road which takes local traffic from Grinkle into South Loftus. It is a heavily wooded district although when I called, much of Warren Wood had been felled.

From Handale, however, there are expansive views towards the sea which lies some three miles to the north.

England's highest cliffs stand on that coastline – they are Boulby Cliffs which are 666 feet high, while nearby is Scaling Reservoir, the largest area of inland water within the North York Moors. It has fishing, boating, watersports and is rich with wildlife. The main bulk of the moors lies to the south of Handale and this reservoir.

In the twelfth century, Handale was the location of a small priory of Benedictine nuns. It was founded in 1133 by Richard de Percy and was dedicated to the Blessed Virgin Mary. Richard de Percy gave the nuns two tofts, ten acres of land and common pasture for two hundred sheep. The abbey continued to thrive until the Reformation when it had eight nuns and the land then passed into the custody of a Mr Ambrose Beckwith. The last of the Beckwiths, Roger, sold it to a Mr Sanderson of Staithes (was this the man to whom young Captain Cook was apprenticed? See chapter twenty-six) and through marriage, it passed into the ownership of the Stephenson family, but no ruins now remain: a farm stands on the site.

There is no village of Handale, but there is an enduring piece of folklore concerning a dragon or, as one old account describes it, 'a loathly worm'. This was one of several such monsters known locally as worms or serpents. There are accounts of others in the chapters on Nunnington, Sexhow and Slingsby.

This serpent had a particularly awesome power over maidens because it was able to lure them into its lair where it kept them for several days before feasting upon them. Many beautiful maids from nearby Loftus had been lured away by the serpent, never to be seen again. It would leave its lair in Handale and journey to Loftus (then called 'Lofthous' or 'Lofthouse') in search of its prey. The moment a maiden set eyes upon this ghastly creature, she was captivated and would then follow it back to Handale. There was no escape, for the huge serpent hypnotized its captives with its large eyes to compel them to follow to its lair. The local people were terrified and none would venture into Handale to kill the beast.

One day a brave hero did arrive from a distant place. He

was called Scaw. He was a handsome, strong and capable young man, and, being a virile sort of chap, he yearned for fair maidens. He quickly realized that there was a scarcity in Loftus and discovered the reason – it wasn't other handsome young men who were taking the maidens away, but a fearsome serpent that lived in a cave. Upon being told this news, Scaw decided to do something about it. He equipped himself with the finest suit of armour that was available, and the keenest sword that could be manufactured, then set about the terrible task of removing the serpent.

As he began his long, dangerous walk into Handale, he was cheered on his way by the good people of Loftus, many of whom had lost their daughters to the serpent.

Some were in tears, some were overcome by his bravery and he was perhaps encouraged by the news that the Lord of the Manor, Richard de Beckwith, had only yesterday lost his own daugher, Emma. She had vanished and it was thought that the serpent had enticed her to its lair. If so, her fate was sealed. When he arrived in Handale, Scaw had then to locate the cave. He must do so before the serpent saw him, for he needed to surprise the beast if he was to achieve victory.

And so the brave Scaw marched through the thick and dangerous wood, seeking the cave which no man had seen. It took a long time, for there were many caves to examine and many tracks to explore. He halted many times to listen, hoping to hear the serpent hissing and finally, as dusk began to envelop the countryside, he heard terrible sounds which could come only from such a creature. The noise came from a large and deep cave at the distant side of a woodland clearing. A steep and rocky cliff faced him and at its base a dark, gaping cavern indicated the serpent's lair: the sounds came from inside. If he were to succeed, Scaw knew he must tempt the serpent into the open and so he bawled and shouted at the cave's entrance, striking the stones with the flat of his sword's blade and so that the sound rang within the depths. And then came terror. With a fearsome roar accompanied by fiery spitting with flames and smoke, the angry serpent of Handale bolted from its lair fully intent on devouring Scaw.

Fortunately, Scaw had anticipated this. He had moved to shelter among the trees and the serpent, its baleful eyes never leaving the young man, followed. Its huge body thrashed and battered the weaker trees to the ground as Scaw made full use of the stout oaks and larger rocks for shelter and protection. But he did not flee from the serpent; he circled it, taunting it by ringing his sword on the boulders of the region, shouting and tempting it into a position in which he could strike it.

The agile, fire-breathing serpent proved not an easy target. Its hot breath seared Scaw's armour making it almost impossible to remain within this protective suit; it almost blinded him with its smoke and awful breath while the thrashing of the huge body tore down cascades of smaller trees, some missing the ever-moving Scaw by a hair's breadth. From time to time, he did manage to slash it with his sword, but the creature's hide was so tough that it made little or no impact. Scaw had to find a vulnerable part of its body – its eyes perhaps, or some softer part. Through this constant movement, Scaw, strong and nimble as he was, was rapidly tiring. He stumbled on one occasion and fell behind a huge boulder, scrambling to safety a fraction of a second before the massive jaws opened to devour him and then, as darkness enveloped Handale, he became utterly exhausted.

He tripped over the branches of a fallen tree and lay wearily as the monster approached to impale him with its fearsome poisoned fangs. Scaw turned onto his back and, at that moment, the serpent presented him with a perfect target. As the huge head came down upon him, Scaw made a final upward thrust with his sword and it pierced the soft throat, severing a blood vessel. The serpent fell dead at his side. Tired almost beyond endurance, Scaw managed to chop off its ugly head just to make sure of victory.

It took him some time to recover any strength, but

before leaving Handale, he decided to examine that lair, remembering that Emma Beckwith was possibly a captive. Dark as it was, he could see her white dress as she cowered in a corner of the stinking cavern, terrified almost beyond belief. Tenderly, Scaw took her hand and led her outside where he showed her the remains of the serpent. As they walked back to Loftus, he fell in love with the delightful fair-haired maiden.

The story has an even happier ending because Scaw wanted to marry the lovely Emma and so he did, with much rejoicing among his friends and the people of the district. Everyone was now free from the ravages of the monster, and Scaw's bravery had won him a most beautiful wife. They married and lived happily ever after. When Peter de Beckwith died, Scaw inherited all the lands and the estate and so he became a rich and famous landowner.

Many years later, long after Scaw had died, a stone coffin was found at the site of Handale Priory. It bore a carved sword on the lid and was said to contain the body of Scaw. It remained on view in Handale up to a century or so ago.

A wood in the area, said to be the one which contained the serpent's lair, was known as Scaw's Wood for many years.

13   Hawsker

Where arrows fell

Hawsker stands upon a wide expanse of land on top of the cliffs about three miles south-east of Whitby town centre. There is a village called High Hawsker which straddles the A171 Whitby – Scarborough road, and a secondary hamlet known as Little Hawsker which is only half a mile away. Hawsker Bottoms, with its stunning coastal views, is near the cliff tops while only a mile or so further south is the romantically named Robin Hood's Bay. Some old names for Hawsker included 'Haukesgard' and 'Haukesgarth', and although some erroneously refer to this area as 'Hawkser', the correct name is 'Hawsker'. In spite of the spelling, it might have come from an Old Norse name meaning 'Hawk's enclosure', hawk coming from a personal name of 'Haukr'.

The area between Hawsker and Whitby Abbey is generally known as Whitby Laithes, 'Laythes' or 'Lathes', an old word referring to an administrative district, although in Yorkshire the term 'lathe' referred to a barn. Once, this district was the manor of Whitby Laithes.

The nineteenth-century parish church of All Saints with its curious tower, stands apart from both Hawskers and is beside a minor road which leads to Whitby Abbey along a route which avoids the 199 steps and the town streets. The church grounds enjoy expansive views of the abbey, the town and the sea. The church is comparatively modern (1877) but has a chimney rising curiously through the roof of the nave with no corresponding fireplace beneath.

In the village, there is an old windmill which adds an air of mystique to the area while a little further exploration will reveal Rigg Mill with its old waterwheel and Cock Mill with a waterfall nearby, together with some delightful wooded areas. There are many caravan sites hereabouts too, some on spectacular cliff-top locations.

The Hawsker cliffs offer stunning seaviews which can be enjoyed from the long-distance Cleveland Way footpath as it clings to the coastline at this point. The rocks below have caused the end of many a passing ship. On the cliffs nearby was the infamous 'Hawsker Bull', the nickname for the fog horn which warned shipping of sea mists.

A cross shaft, some six feet tall, stands in the grounds of Hall Farm at Hawsker. It depicts a bird and a dragon and other Viking or Saxon motifs, suggesting it dates from around the first half of the eleventh century. It suggests a chapel of some kind on this site around the eleventh century, probably built by Asketil, a monk of Whitby Abbey.

But it is two other standing stones that link Hawsker to the many stories of Robin Hood and his Merry Men. It is widely reported that, when sorely pressed by the King's men or by the Sheriff of Nottingham, Robin Hood would flee to Robin Hood's Bay (see chapter nineteen), very close to Hawsker.

There he would escape his pursuers with help from local people. He spent many happy hours in the area, sometimes on the cliffs near Hawsker, sometimes inland and in the forests and on the moors, and sometimes fishing in the bay which now bears his name. And, if the legend has any substance at all, one of his favourite calling places was Whitby Abbey where the abbot was a good friend of the outlaw, perhaps seeing in Robin the potential for conversion.

On a brisk and chilly day in March, therefore, Robin Hood and Little John were enjoying a carefree day hunting cliff foxes which roamed the area. These were alert and cunning animals which destroyed the poultry and geese of tenant farmers and landowners. Robin and John hunted alone; they had no hounds and they were neither dressed in the manner of the huntsmen of the period nor in the famous Lincoln green. Instead, they were in anonymous garments, looking like labourers of the district.

It was an effective disguise for none would have recognized the country's most famous outlaw and his friend. The local people did know them, of course, but they would never reveal their whereabouts or their identity to any soldier or official. Their secret was safe in the hands of the Hawsker folk and the people of Whitby Laithes. Had any outsider observed the archery skills of the pair, however, then some suspicions might have been raised, for it must have been clear to even the most unobservant that these were no ordinary bowmen.

From time to time, they competed with one another, shooting at tiny objects in the distance and scoring hits every time or alternatively positioning several arrows in one small target such as a mark on a tree stump or in the timber of a barn door. They even killed running foxes with well-aimed arrows and then handed the carcases to the owners or tenants of the land. In successive hunts, Robin Hood and Little John killed many marauding foxes and lots of cottages around Whitby Laithes used to display masks and brushes of reynards shot by Robin Hood and Little John. These trophies were proudly handed down from generation to generation.

On this day in March, their hunting took them towards the abbey of St Hilda. They had started around 5 a.m. and had put up many daring animals; some had fallen to the longbows of both Robin and Little John while others had managed to evade the skilled pair. But hunger was gnawing at the bellies of the hunters. In March, there was no fruit to pick but Robin and Little John knew the brethren of the abbey would never turn them away; they were long-term friends of Abbot Richard, having met in Peterborough. And, furthermore, did not the abbey's poultry and game need protection from foxes? It was a service Robin cheerfully exchanged for an occasional bowl of hot game soup and some slices of venison cooked to perfection.

And so, around eleven that morning, they made their way through the mighty portals to be welcomed by the guestmaster, Brother William. They had brought the mask of a fox, evidence of their current mission, and in the guest room, before a blazing log fire, they drank wine from the abbey's cellars as they awaited their meal. At eleven thirty, they were shown into the long refectory which lay to the south of the abbey church; there, a monk was at the lectern reading aloud from the gospels. The meal, after prayers, would be in silence as was the tradition, and, as they ate, the words of today's gospel would fill the large room. At the end of the long oak table, there would be extra places – these were always available for travellers and guests, whether anticipated or not, for no abbey would turn away those in need of rest and refreshment.

After a blessing by Abbot Richard, Robin Hood and Little John settled down to their meal; there was a hot, spicy broth with large chunks of hot bread followed by a beef stew liberally laced with vegetables. Apples gathered last autumn from the abbey's extensive orchards and still fresh from the cool store, followed with figs and raisins from a finger bowl, then a beaker of ale and several glasses of wine. After the grace which followed, Abbot Richard indicated that he would walk for half an hour in the grounds with Robin and Little John. Perhaps, in a moment of light relief, this meeting resulted in a curious challenge between Robin Hood and Little John. It seems that the talks did broach the subject of archery, for the challenge was to determine which of these superb bowmen could shoot furthest from the highest point of Whitby Abbey. This spontaneous sporting event was to be witnessed not only by the abbot, but also by the entire brethren.

Abbot Richard was proud of his abbey, for his efforts had produced several new buildings within its confines, one of which was a massive tower. On that windy day, therefore, he and the two famous outlaws climbed that tower and emerged on the roof, there to survey the landscape before commencement of the contest. It was far too dangerous to shoot arrows to the south and west, for those areas were rich with cottages and harm might be done to passersby. To the north there was only the sea and indeed, the cliffs also drew close to the east. But stretching across Whitby Laithes to the south-east was a long lane bounded by high hedges and open fields; it led from the abbey via the old Manor House of Whitby Laithes and into the village of Haukesgard (now called Hawsker).

'If you shoot in that direction it will be safe,' shouted Abbot Richard above the roar of the wind. 'We will all be able to follow the path of your arrows and trace their fall.'

Having determined the battleground and that no one was walking along Stainsacre Lane or in the neighbouring fields, the abbot gave his consent for the contest to begin. Each would fire ten arrows in turn, Robin's being identified by red fletching and Little John's by blue. Several monks on horseback were positioned at intervals along the lane to act as umpires and the contest would begin by the wave of a flag from the tower roof.

Little John began. His first arrow soared from the roof and over the high walls of the abbey to land in a field to the south of the lane near Stoupe Cross; it was marked by a monk. Robin shot next, his first arrow landing very close to John's albeit to the north of the lane. It was perhaps two yards further than John's. All the following five arrows from each man landed in roughly this position, and then John fired a mighty shot. As he released his arrow, a gust of the blustery north-westerly wind blew from the sea and caught the feathers of the slender arrow to make it rise like a kite. The moment was exactly right, the timing of the shot was perfect. John's arrow rose over the portals of the huge abbey and soared like a bird towards Haukesgard. The monks gasped and cheered as the blue arrow flew effortlessly away and it was almost out of sight before dipping towards the earth along Whitby Laithes. It fell just short of a moat which surrounded the abbey's lands. A monk raced to the place and stood there, waving his arms and shouting his astonishment: it was a colossal shot, a miracle of archery.

Now it was Robin's turn, but the wind had dropped. Robin's sixth shot fell well short of that enormous distance and so did John's seventh. None of John's remaining arrows reached the distance and neither did any of Robin's until it was time for his final attempt – his reputation depended upon this last shot and it seemed that only a miracle, or a renewal of that fresh wind, would enable him to beat John's remarkable effort.

Robin Hood, hero of the poor and the nation's most famous outlaw, therefore stood on the highest point of Whitby Abbey with his final arrow in position. He could see the monk dwarfed in the distance, as he stood beside that miraculous arrow of Little John. But Robin Hood was an archer of superb quality, a man with a steady arm and a keen eye and as he waited in those tense moments, the wind arose once more. It whistled through the stones of the abbey, rising around the mighty walls and Robin knew he must take advantage of its strength. He could see the sea birds wheeling and soaring on the rising currents and, with all senses alert and waiting for precisely the right moment, he released his final arrow.

With a cry of delight and surprise from the assembly, the red arrow rose into the sky in the manner of Little John's and they saw that it was taking the same path, flying ahead of the powerful gust that had been so well harnessed by Robin.

But, as the arrow began its descent, it was clear that it would fall short of Little John's record. And so it did. It fell to the south of Stainsacre Lane only a couple of yards short of little John's. Robin Hood congratulated his old friend and rival, and thanked the abbot and community for arranging this contest. After a celebratory glass of wine, the two outlaws left the abbey to continue hunting, with Robin saying there would be further challenges between the friends.

The abbot, however, was not going to allow such a tremendous demonstration of archery to go unremarked.

He ordered that two stones be erected at the places where the arrows fell, one to mark Little John's winning arrow and the other to mark Robin Hood's. Within days, a four-foot-tall stone pillar marked Robin's arrow while a similar one, two and a half feet tall, marked Little John's. The fields where the other arrows fell became known as Little John's Close and Robin Hood's Close, and were still registered as such, along with the location of those stones, in records dated 1713.

By 1890, those two stones had been removed because they were in the way of mowing machines, so 'Robin Hood' and 'Little John' were unceremoniously uprooted and dumped in a ditch, later to be photographed by the famous Whitby photographer Frank Meadow Sutcliffe. He persuaded a farmer to re-erect Robin Hood for the sake of the photograph. Later, in 1937, one of these stones was being used as a field roller near Hawsker Church.

Today, however, a pair of replacement stones identifies the site of those arrows. Each stone is around two feet high with a top wider than its base. One bears the name Robin Hood and the other Little John, his being six feet or so further from the abbey. They were erected in 1903 and stand beside the public footpath that leads from Manor Farm on Whitby Laithes towards the A171 across Stainsacre Lane. They are about 100 yards from Stainsacre Lane and provide an open view of Whitby Abbey. The distance from these stones to the abbey is about 1 mile, 660 yards, but there can be no guarantee they occupy the positions of the earlier stones.

If they do, then, would such a long-distance shot be possible, bearing in mind it was from an elevated position with an assisting wind? According to the *Guinness Book of Records*, the longest distance ever shot, in the unlimited footbow class, was 1 mile, 268 yards, shot at ground level. The greatest distance using a handbow at ground level was 1,231½ yards, a shade more than three quarters of a mile.

It is pleasing to think that, in these circumstances, Robin Hood and Little John, the nation's greatest exponents of the bow and arrow, could have shot over this distance.

14   The Hole of Horcum

The Devil's Punchbowl

One of the outstanding visual attractions of the North
York Moors is the Hole of Horcum. It is a huge, deep
hollow, large enough to accommodate a couple of farms
and their fields, as well as to provide the watershed of
Levisham Beck. From its marshy basin, several gills and
ponds pour water into Levisham Beck which eventually
joins Pickering Beck at Farwath in Newtondale.

The A169 Pickering-to-Whitby road skirts the eastern
edge and a spacious car-park provides ample opportunity
to savour the incredible views and to ponder over the
formation of this intriguing chasm. In the distance, the
valley carries the North York Moors steam railway from
Goathland to Pickering, using a route which opened in
May 1836, only the third passenger line to be created in
the country. So marshy was the route that a foundation
was made from trees, and heather bound in sheepskins.
The rails were laid on top and, even today, there might be
a reminder of these spongy foundations in the gentle
up-and-down motion of the moving train. A ride on this
steam railway provides a vivid reminder of the line's past
glories and is a wonderful means of savouring the
splendours of the moors.

Nearby are the Bridestones, curiously shaped outcrops
of sandstone which are within the National Trust's
Bridestones Nature Reserve. Access is through the Dalby
Forest Drive which is well sign-posted, and a small charge
is made.

The rim of the Hole of Horcum has become popular with hang gliders as well as motorists, hikers and other sightseers. The steep, winding road drops from the summit to strike across the moors towards Whitby. In the distance can be seen the distinctive outlines of Fylingdales Ballistic Missile Early Warning Station, a reminder that we are in the final years of the twentieth century even if the surrounding moors echo with the signs of ages past.

One of the legendary associations with the Hole of Horcum is the hill which takes traffic past the remote Saltersgate Inn. It is called the Devil's Elbow, a name perhaps created by the drivers of horse-drawn coaches who had to negotiate it during all kinds of weather. The inn used to be a coaching halt and there was once a toll gate here; the inn was also the haunt of salt smugglers, hence its name, and it boasts a peat fire that has been alight since 1800. It is not allowed to go out and was used for making turf cakes; but this ancient fire, in its marvellous surrounds, can also boast links with the Devil.

One ancient folk story tells how the Devil was crossing these moors during a chilly and inhospitable night and he decided to call at the Saltersgate Inn for warmth and food.

He was recognized and received a very hostile reception, the leader of which was a priest who chanced to be at the inn. The priest exorcized the premises, but rather than flee outside in the awful weather, the Devil sought sanctuary in the kitchen. A peat fire was immediately lit to keep him there, and so long as that fire burns, the Devil will not enter any other part of the inn: he is trapped by the smouldering peat. The fire continues to burn even today but, due to alterations, it is now in the bar area.

Another tale surrounding that fire is that there was a battle between some fishermen of Robin Hood's Bay who were salt smugglers and a Whitby excise man who was trying to convict them. As they illegally salted their fish in the cellars, he crept in to catch them and a tremendous fight ensued. He was killed and hastily buried under the fireplace, the perpetrators hoping the authorities would think he had perished on the moors. A new fireplace was installed in 1800 by Dobsons of Pickering and, it is said that, the fire has never been allowed to go out just in case someone tries to discover what lies beneath it. Perhaps the local people concocted the story of the Devil to deter anyone from investigating the theories of that old fireside, and another belief is that if the peat fire is allowed to die out, then the ghost of the dead excise man will return to haunt the premises.

It is the Devil who is also said to be responsible for the Hole of Horcum. Ancient tradition says that he scooped out a handful of earth and threw it across the moors; the hollow that remained is now the Hole of Horcum, or the 'Devil's Punchbowl' as some still call it, while the heap which he cast aside became Blakey Topping. This is an 800-feet-high hill about a mile to the east of the Hole of Horcum, although some say that either Freeborough Hill (see chapter six) or Roseberry Topping (see chapter twenty) were also formed by a giant handful of earth thrown from here. This tale is reinforced by an old notion that the marks of the Devil's fingers can be seen in the slopes of the Hole of Horcum and, curiously enough, the contour lines at the base of the hole even now form the shape of a fist with a finger pointing to the south-west!

Yet another claim about the source of the Hole of Horcum says that it is the work of the giant Wade. He is said to have scooped handfuls of earth from here, either to make his famous Causeway across the moors (see chapter twenty-nine) or to throw at his enemies. In truth, it is a natural depression, probably the work of countless tiny streams and springs which, over the ages, have carried away the softer soil to create this incredible hole in the ground.

The source of the name remains a real puzzle – in the thirteenth century, it was known as 'Hotcumbe' and later as 'Holcumbe', becoming 'Horcumbe' or 'Horcombe' after 1326. By 1500, it was known as 'Horkome' and there might be links through the Old English language, with 'Urra Moor'.

'Urra' and 'Hor' may derive from the Old English word *horh*, which means filth. Perhaps the name, therefore, comes from the marshy quality of the floor of the Hole of Horcum? Or did the Devil throw the contents of the Hole of Horcum across the moors to create Urra Moor, at 1490 feet, the highest point of the North York Moors?

15 Kettleness

The Claymore Well bogles

Kettleness is noted for its sea views, as the hamlet sits among spectacular cliff-top scenery between Whitby and Staithes. It is less than a mile from Goldsborough, another cliff-top community, both of which can be reached through narrow lanes which lead off the A174. The old coastal railway line between Middlesbrough and Whitby passed nearby, and the long-distance footpath, the Cleveland Way, hugs the cliffs to the seaward side of Kettleness.

Goldsborough is a lonely windswept place with a tiny inn but it does boast a history dating from the Romans. They had a chain of signalling stations along this coast, one of which was at Goldsborough. It was beside the lane which leads to Kettleness and, in the fifth century, it was ransacked and its occupants assassinated. In 1919, the site was excavated and skulls, clothing and coins were discovered, along with an entire human skeleton and some animal bones including those of a dog. The signalling station had outer defences comprising a twelve-feet-wide ditch outside its wall which was five feet thick.

Kettleness comprises a handful of cottages and a coastguard station above Kettleness Point, a 400-feet-high cliff. In 1829, some of the cliff slid into the North Sea, taking with it the entire hamlet. The slide was gentle, however, for the inhabitants had time to reach the safety of an alum ship standing off shore. They were saved although their homes were lost. This was just one of many landslides in this area. In 1857, the fossilized remains of an ichthyosaurus and a plesiosaurus were found here while the entire area is rich with folklore and legend.

Near Goldsborough are two standing stones; they are almost a mile apart and each is known as Wade's Stone. These are associated with the Saxon giant Wade (see chapter twenty-nine) while further along the coast there lived the Runswick Hob (see chapter twenty-one) and also the bogle known as Jeannie of Mulgrave Wood (see chapter sixteen).

Kettleness has its own bogles. A bogle is a type of mischievous goblin or hob-goblin, sprite, pixie or elf; there are others of similar ilk who are known as boggarts or even puckles. From puckle we get the name Puck and there are still more creatures of this sort, such as brownies, kelpies, hobs and even Robin Goodfellow. Several existed in and around the North York Moors, notably hobs, bogles and fairies. The name bogle appears in some locations, such as Boggle Hole on the coast near Robin Hood's Bay, and in the name of a house called Boggle House between Grosmont and Goathland. The double 'g' is a local variation of the spelling. So far as the Kettleness bogles are concerned, no one seems quite sure what they looked like.

Were they little brown elves or small hairy goblins or merely a community of charming fairies? Sightings are rare or non-existent, but it is known they lived at Claymore Well which is about a mile to the east of Kettleness and Goldsborough. It is a few yards from Hob Holes in the cliffs near Runswick Bay, itself the haunt of a hob (see chapter twenty-one), so may we assume that the noises made by the hob were the same that the Kettleness folk attributed to bogles? Maybe the bogles of Kettleness and the hob of Runswick Bay are one and the same?

What the Kettleness folk heard was what 'everybody used to ken': that bogles lived at Claymore Well and could be heard washing and bleaching their clothes. They would beat them with an old-fashioned implement known as a 'battledore'; this was a wooden object rather like the paddle of a canoe with a long handle and a circular, flat blade. It was used by washerwomen for smoothing their linen, but fell into disuse when the powerful mangle came along to ease their labours. The bogles of Claymore Well used to set aside one night a week for their washing, and the noise of them using their battledores to beat their clothes with a curious rhythm would fill the night air around Kettleness.

No one, however, ventured that way to peep at the bogles during this work, and so no reliable account exists.

16   Lythe

Jeannie of Mulgrave Wood

Lythe is a hill-top village on the A174 overlooking the coastline four miles north-east of Whitby. It stands on the summit of Lythe Bank, a long, steep hill which carries the main road into Sandsend and boasts remarkable sea views.

Lythe's sturdy parish church of St Oswald is worth a visit. There was a church here in Saxon times and the present building has long survived fierce sea storms. One of its former priests was later to become a cardinal in the Roman Catholic church. He was the distinguished scholar and bishop, John Fisher, later St John Fisher, who defied Henry VIII at the Reformation and so paid with his life. In 1534, while he was in prison, he was created cardinal by Pope Paul III but was executed on Tower Hill, London, on 22 June 1535. He was canonized in 1935. The church is now Anglican.

Of interest in the churchyard is a memorial to seven unknown sailors. Their bodies were washed ashore below the church during the first World War and they have never been identified.

In the centre of the village is a blacksmith's forge, a tiny building very close to the main road and almost opposite the Red Lion Inn. The anvil can be seen through the window. This is the scene of an old custom known as 'Firing the Stiddy', a stiddy being an anvil.

It celebrates notable events in the family of the Marquis

of Normanby who live in the beautiful Mulgrave Castle at Lythe. The stiddy was fired in 1951 to celebrate the wedding of the present Marquis and Marchioness of Normanby, in 1954 to mark the birth of their eldest son, in 1971 to honour the visit by helicopter of the Duchess of Gloucester and in 1975 to mark the coming of age of the Earl of Mulgrave. For the ceremonial, the stiddy is carried outside and wooden plugs are primed with gunpowder, then fired on the stiddy with a twenty-foot long iron rod, heated in the fire of the blacksmith's shop.

The core of the castle was built around 1735 by Catherine, Duchess of Buckingham, a natural daughter of James II, and it has since been extended and rendered more beautiful, much of it in early Georgian style. A summer-house in the grounds marks the site of a hermitage built in 1150 by William de Percy. The modern castle stands on the edge of a deep, wooded ravine containing a large selection of deciduous trees. These are Mulgrave Woods in which there are the remains of a much earlier castle, sometimes called Foss Castle, which dates from the Norman conquest. One of its occupants was the legendary giant Wade (see chapter twenty-nine) who lived here with his wife, Bell. Also in these woods are the Devil's Bridge, Wizard's Glen, Eagle's Nest and the Waterfall, all giving some indication of the mystical atmosphere which prevails.

Mulgrave Castle has been host to many very important visitors including members of the Royal family. Charles Dickens also enjoyed a stay; it is said he danced on the lawns with ecstasy! He later dedicated his novel, *Dombey and Son*, 'with great esteem to the Marchioness of Normanby'.

Below Lythe is the pretty village of Sandsend, aptly named for its nestles on the very edge of the sea. On the site of a Roman cement works, it is now a cluster of charming cottages at the end of two and a half miles of golden sands extending to Whitby.

Such a fascinating part of Yorkshire is sure to have lore and legends, and so it has. In addition to being the focus of stories about the giant Wade, Lythe has its own legend, the story of a sprite called Jeannie. Some accounts say she was a good fairy with a notoriously bad temper whenever anyone upset her; another account suggests that she was really an evil witch or female goblin. Whatever her true nature, Jeannie was blamed by the farmers if anything went wrong with their crops or farm animals. At times, they wondered what had upset her so much that she wreaked vengeance upon them and their produce. It seems, however, that one of her great desires was to remain in seclusion, for she was very shy and hated inquisitive visitors.

As a consequence, very few saw Jeannie so we have no recorded description of her. We do not know whether she was large or small, fat or thin, ugly or pretty; we do not know whether she looked like an elf, a hob or a witch with a large hooked nose. In short, Jeannie is a mystery.

Inevitably, this lack of knowledge excited a good deal of interest but no one dared try to find her home in case she became angry. Everyone, with one exception, allowed Jeannie to live her life undisturbed. The exception was a young man called John Roe. Like many other young men, he worked on his father's farm and had heard of Jeannie. As a child, he had been told she lived in a cave called Hob Cave deep in Mulgrave Woods, and he wondered whether Jeannie was a beautiful young woman. He had heard stories of her terrible anger but equally, had been told of her charms. He believed that Jeannie was a lovely, peaceful fairy, so gentle in her manners and so quiet in her way of life that she might make a fine wife for a hard-working lad ...

John Roe convinced himself that he would make Jeannie a good husband. He also reckoned such a union would end those terrible bouts of destructive anger for which she was feared. He decided to pay her a visit. Late one summer evening, therefore, after turning the hay, he told his parents that he was going to the inn to join his friends for a drink. He saddled his horse and rode off. Instead John was going to visit Jeannie. He knew he would have difficulty locating her cave for no one had seen it. He would make a meticulous search instead of trusting to chance and began at the lower end of Mulgrave Woods, close to the beach at Sandsend.

He worked his way through the dense undergrowth and leafy glades, checking every outcrop of rock, every hillside and every concealed place. He removed briars and undergrowth, he startled animals and birds and he must have cut down many square yards of vegetation during that search. It took him deep into the woods until he came to a place not far from the ruins of Foss Castle. And there, shielded by a tangled growth of blackberry bushes and honeysuckle, was the entrance to a large cave. And it was clearly inhabited: he saw the signs of a fire outside, some cooking utensils and a three-legged stool. John Roe had found Hob Cave, the secret and legendary home of Jeannie of Mulgrave Woods.

Dusk had arrived and it was very dark inside the cave. A tangle of briars prevented him from peering into its secret depths, so he dismounted for a closer look. Hardly had his feet touched the ground when a fearsome creature bolted out of that cave, shrieking and screaming and waving a long wand. There was a flurry of arms and legs, a scattering of leaves and the birds of the woods took to their wings in terror as animals fled for their lives. So did John Roe.

He clambered aboard his horse and spurred it into a gallop as he fled from the awful screaming and flailing creature, but Jeannie gave chase. He looked behind and saw, with horror, that she was almost floating through the woods and so he whipped his horse into a frenzy as it crashed through the trees and shrubs, desperately seeking a way out.

The terrible Jeannie was gaining ground. As the gallant horse did its desperate best to find an exit, so the shrieking figure, as large as John himself, scratched and clawed at the headquarters of the horse and attempted to seize John by the throat … His horse could outpace Jeannie on the long straight paths, but there were so few; every route seemed to be narrow and winding with rocks abounding and gulleys to traverse as he fled, head down on the neck of his horse. He was fleeing for his life, when he suddenly remembered a piece of folklore told to him by his grandmother many years ago: 'Fairies will not cross water,' his aged granny had said. 'Allus you remember that, young John.'

Now he did remember it, with gratitude. Several streams flowed through Mulgrave Woods including the sparkling Mickleby Beck and the fast-flowing East Row Beck with its many tributaries. There were lots of suitable streams if only he could reach one ....

Just as Jeannie had gained on the horse during a difficult stretch, so John noticed a stream before him. It glistened in the half-light and he urged his tiring horse towards it. There was a low cliff, he noticed, and knew he could use it as a launching point for leaping the beck. He arrived just as Jeannie, still screaming and flailing her arms, had reached his horse. With a super-human effort, he whipped his weary horse into a colossal leap, but Jeannie had anticipated his actions.

With a blood-curdling yell, she brought down her wand on the rear of the horse and it fell in mid-air, as dead as a dry leaf. As the poor animal rolled lifeless into the stream, John fell clear as the defeated Jeannie stood and shrieked at the edge of the water. John was safe and scrambled ashore, dripping wet and bruised from the fall. He ran for his life, with perspiration falling from him as he fled through the wood; he had to leave his gallant horse dead in the saving water.

He arrived home, wet, tired and utterly terrified, and it was several hours before he could gasp out the story of his experience. He never went back to Mulgrave Woods and, since that time, no one else has tried to find Jeannie's cave.

She is never disturbed and so the crops around Lythe flourish and the farm animals live peacefully without fear of her wrath.

17 Nunnington

The Nunnington Worm

Nunnington is a charming Ryedale village a couple of miles beyond the southern boundary of the North York Moors National Park. Its peaceful situation just off Helmsley-Malton road (B1257) means that a high proportion of traffic passes by in spite of the undoubted attractions. With its ancient yellow limestone houses bearing red pantile roofs, and its quiet location on the banks of the River Rye, it presents the ideal hideaway for tourists and city visitors.

Its sights include an eighteenth-century bridge across the River Rye, some delightful seventeenth-century almshouses (close to Nunnington Hall), a striking avenue of sycamores said to be the haunt of a ghost, the parish church of All Saints and St James and the imposing Nunnington Hall.

The Hall stands in beautiful gardens on the banks of the Rye and occupies the site of a former nunnery. It dates from two periods. Parts can be dated from 1552 when built by the squire, John Hickes, and other portions are mainly seventeenth century when alterations were carried out by Viscount Preston, the noted Stuart supporter. He became Secretary of State for Scotland under James II, but was later charged with treason. He escaped the death penalty by betraying some of his confederates.

The Hall contains a magnificent panelled hall with a wonderful carved chimneypiece; the bedrooms are panelled too and the furnishings include some fine tapestries and china. The famous Carlisle Collection of Miniature Rooms is lodged here; these are fully furnished models and are a delight. This former home of Viscount Preston and the Graham family is now administered by the National Trust and is open to the public, the times depending upon the season.

The parish church on its hilltop site is a restored version of a thirteenth-century structure; much was rebuilt after the Reformation, the tower being dated as 1672. Inside are fragments of a tenth-century stone cross, one of which bears part of a dragon, and in the south wall of the nave, in a recess, is the effigy of a knight. This is probably Sir Walter de Teye who died in 1325; he is clad in armour, his legs are crossed, he holds a heart in his hands and at his feet is the figure of a lion. The carved dragon and the tomb of Sir Walter are reminders of a remarkable legend, for some believe that the tomb is really that of a local hero, Sir Peter Loschi, and that the lion is really Sir Peter's dog. The story of Sir Peter and his dog, and their defeat of the ghastly Nunnington Worm, is part of the village's folk history.

The story begins on St Barnabas Day, 11 June, during a year long before William the Conqueror came to the British Isles. This was before the calendar changes which declared 24 June to be Mid Summer day. At that time, 11 June was Mid Summer day.

By tradition, it was when the hay was gathered in, and was dedicated to St Barnabas, himself a farm labourer. The day was known as Barnaby Bright and an old verse said:

> Barnaby bright, Barnaby bright,
> Longest day and shortest night.

After the hay had been gathered in, the people of Nunnington celebrated by lighting a bonfire on a hill top close to where the church now stands. As the flames grew stronger, people began to gather, for here was music and dancing with a feast of good things. The merry-making continued into the early hours and all the workers and their families travelled miles to enjoy the festivities. They came from Stonegrave, East Newton, Ness and other nearby hamlets.

The older folk were sitting around the fire, enjoying the occasion and meeting old friends while the youngsters danced and sang, with flirtations and romances highlighting the occasion. One important event was the crowning of the Barnaby Queen. The selection had been made by a group of youngsters – she was a beautiful fifteen-year-old maiden called Frances Mortain. According to old accounts, she had a beautiful fair complexion, flaxen curls and soft blue eyes which caused all the youths to fall in love with her. The custom was to transport the Barnaby Queen on a cart loaded with new hay; this was the symbolic final load and it was drawn by a white horse decorated with ribbons and flanked by six young bachelors.

This small procession was the highlight of the evening and was supposed to travel from a point near the river up to the blazing bonfire. On this night, therefore, six youths assembled beside the cart, three on each side; Frances was on top of the load in her white dress with a crown of brilliant summer flowers on her head and a posy in her hand. At a signal, the cart began its journey. On the hill, the fire was stoked anew and flames and sparks shot into the evening sky as the people sang and danced and clapped their hands while awaiting their Barnaby Queen.

Even as the procession was making its way up the steep hill, however, horror was about to descend upon the merrymaking. A terrible hissing sound filled the sky; it was like thousands of angry geese and in the glow of fire, the people saw a giant serpent snaking across the fields. It had the head of a dragon and the body of a massive reptile as flames burst from its mouth and nostrils. The village was filled with screams and cries of fear as it rapidly approached and, within seconds, everyone fled from the scene. The only person unable to flee was poor Frances. She was marooned on top of the wagon-load of hay. She lay down flat, hoping the oncoming monster would never catch sight of her, but it did.

With remarkable speed and agility, it wrapped its coils about her fragile body and carried her off, screaming with fear and pain. It carried her to its lair on Loschi Hill between Stonegrave and Nunnington. No one dared to follow.

In the past, some youths had tried to kill the monster but none had succeeded. Only one local hero was capable of undertaking that task, and he was away from home. He was Sir Peter Loschi, a Nunnington knight famed for his bravery and gallant deeds. He was a member of King Arthur's knights of the Round Table and spent a lot of time at Queen Guinevere's court, charming the ladies and winning regular contests of skill and strength against other knights. It was only rarely that he returned to his ancestral home at Nunnington.

Fortunately Sir Peter was due for a holiday. He had slain a giant Saxon, defeated several of the King's enemies single-handed, recovered Arthur's standard from a band of felons, rescued lots of damsels from fates worse than death, slaughtered a rampaging lion and killed a dangerous ox, and defeated a dragon, a griffin and even a hippogriff, in addition to many other stirring successes. Weary from these labours, he decided to have a quiet holiday in Nunnington, taking with him his faithful dog. He arrived in the nick of time: the worm had just departed with its victim.

Tired though he was, Sir Peter listened as the villagers recited their tale of woe and he could not refuse their heartfelt pleas for help. Being both clever and brave, he fully appreciated the problems of fighting dragons and similar monsters and so devised a special suit of armour for his forthcoming battle.

It was studded with sharp blades which were the tips of razor-keen swords, and in addition he possessed his own special sword. It had a Damascene blade and included the same ingredients as the famous sword Excalibur used by King Arthur.

These preparations had taken a few days during which time other maidens had been taken by the invading worm but, now rested from his previous labours, Peter was determined to end this continuing harassment. On the day of his battle, therefore, he donned his suit of armour and had great difficulty preventing his dog, a mastiff, from leaping up and injuring itself, but, with a red plume bobbing upon his helmet and his trusty sword at the ready, Sir Peter strode towards the worm's lair. The villagers gathered where Nunnington church stands and watched from a safe distance.

The worm saw him coming and roared into the attack, but Peter was quick. He slashed at it with his sword as his gallant mastiff circled and bit the creature in several places but, each time his sword cut the monster, its flesh instantly healed. Try as he might, Sir Peter could not kill the monster because every stroke of his sword produced a lot of blood but the wounds were to no effect. He and his dog fought for hours and hours. As Sir Peter grew increasingly tired, the serpent coiled itself around his body, cutting itself terribly on the barbs, but each wound healed within moments. Sir Peter was losing his battle, but his brave and intelligent dog came to the rescue.

As a tiny piece of the worm's tail was cut on one of those razor-sharp blades, it fell to the ground; before the wound could heal, the dog seized the piece and carried it off. The worm now roared with pain; it grew fearsomely angry and began to spit masses of poisonous fumes. It uncoiled itself from Sir Peter to attack his dog, and it did so, Peter slashed with his sword, cutting off another piece of body … the dog dashed in and carried that away.

And as the injured monster turned its full attention to the brave mastiff, so Sir Peter's wonderful sword chopped piece after piece from its ailing body. Each time, his dog carried off the portion, so denying the worm its ability to heal itself. Finally, there was only the head left. The dragon issued a final hiss of poisonous fumes and died as the gallant dog carried the head towards the cheering crowd. It deposited this trophy where Nunnington church now stands.

The tired but triumphant Sir Peter examined the lair but

none of the missing maidens remained. All had perished, but no more would become victims of the Nunnington Worm.

As Sir Peter made his triumphant walk back towards the village, his faithful dog leapt up to lick his face – but the dog's breath and its teeth were laced with poison from the worm. Within seconds, Sir Peter Loschi fell, poisoned by the evil juices of the conquered worm, and within moments, his mastiff also collapsed. When the grieving villagers reached them, both were dead; they were later buried together.

Man and dog are honoured forever in Nunnington, for inside the church there is a monument depicting a recumbent knight with a dog at his feet.

18   Pickering

The story of Pereduras' ring

Pickering is reputedly a shy town and in some ways this is true. From a tourist's point of view, it is among the less well known of the charming market towns that encircle the North York Moors and yet it has much to offer. Indeed, it justifiably claims to be 'The Gateway to the Moors', for it lies just outside the boundaries of the National Park.

There is an ancient castle which is almost hidden, the town centre sports an open-air market on Mondays and at the bottom of the market-place there is the terminus of the North York Moors steam railway. In the town centre there is the Kirk Theatre, the Beck Isle Museum of Rural Life, some fascinating inns and shops, and the parish church famed for its gallery of fifteenth-century wall paintings. Near the outskirts, there is Flamingoland Zoo, Castle Howard (famous as the house featured in the television adaptation of *Brideshead Revisited*) and the whole of the North York Moors with the fabulous coastline and resorts like Whitby, Scarborough and Filey. The Yorkshire Wolds and Yorkshire Dales are also within a short drive.

The castle on its hill top site dates from the early years of the Norman conquest when the original was a timber fort. Most of the present building dates from between 1180 to the fourteenth century, and the entrance is fifteenth century. The keep was built around 1220.

The large hall was constructed around 1314 from which

doors lead into the kitchen, buttery and pantry. Inside the grounds are towers such as Colman's Tower, Rosamund's Tower, Diate Hill Tower and Mill Tower, and a chapel dating from 1226.

Pickering Castle has featured in national events – Richard II was imprisoned there before being taken to Pontefract, Henry VII and Richard III have stayed, and Cromwell attacked the castle with his cannons. Between 1100 and 1400, every reigning English king visited the castle to hunt in the nearby Blansby Park, for the huge Forest of Pickering was a royal hunting ground. It stretched from Rosedale across the moors to Eskdale and the coast.

One unproven story concerns Rosamund's Tower. The tower is said to be named after the mistress of Henry II, the fair Rosamund Clifford who, it is said, was imprisoned here. But the tower was constructed a century after her death, so she could never have been within its walls. One theory is that she accompanied the king to Pickering Castle during one of his visits, and that the tower was later named in her honour. Today, Pickering Castle is owned by HM The Queen through the Duchy of Lancaster; it is cared for by the Department of the Environment and is open to the public.

Before being open to the public in its present form, the castle used to open on Easter Day, and at times tennis was played on its lawns and an open-air market held within the walls.

When in Pickering, visitors should examine the interior of the church of St Peter and St Paul which dates to Norman times. Apart from the history contained within the building, the wall paintings are the most complete of any such work in the English churches. They date from the middle of the fifteenth century and were hidden by whitewash until 1851 when restoration revealed them. After unsuccessfully trying to erase them, the vicar immediately tried to conceal them again because he worried that they might be idolatrous, but they were re-discovered in 1878 and now provide a wonderful example of what the interior of a church looked like prior to the Reformation. The paintings depict many events: St George slaying the dragon, St Christopher, Salome carrying the head of John the Baptist, the martyrdom of St Thomas à Becket and other stirring portrayals.

The history of Pickering is uncertain, but is clearly of ancient origins. One historian, Stowe, believed it dated from around 270 BC, when it was founded by Pereduras who was a king of the Britons. Other authorities believe the name means 'the settlement of Picer and his dependants', coming from the Old Norse 'Piceringas'. Even in Norman times, the town was known as 'Pichering', later becoming 'Pikering' and finally Pickering.

There is also a delightful legend which explains how the town received its name. Long ago, before the time of Christ, King Pereduras was swimming in the pond which gives rise to the Costa Beck. It is called Keld Head Spring.

The young king possessed a valuable ring which was an heirloom and he never took it from his finger. But it was easy not to keep on because it had become enlarged and worn, having belonged to his father and his grandfather before him. Thus it was somewhat loose on Pereduras' finger. On a warm, summer day in June, therefore, he chose to swim in Keld Head Spring. He was with some other young princes, men of his own kind and standing, and after the swim, they adjourned to his castle for a meal. His castle stood on the shores of that lake and as he entered his home, he realized that he had lost the precious ring. They all returned to the pond and swam under the water for as long as possible, seeking the ring among the mud and weeds at the bottom, but had no luck. They even searched the clear waters of the Costa Beck, walking and exploring several miles downstream to a second pond near what is now Costa Lodge, but their efforts were in vain. For several months afterwards, Pereduras continued his hunt, but found nothing.

He knew that it was his duty to hand this ring to his son that he might rule the land, and there is little doubt that the loss concerned him greatly.

One day, many years afterwards when he was married and raising his own sons, Pereduras settled down to a fine meal with his family. They still lived in the palace on the shores of that lake and he had caught a pike in the beck. His queen had arranged for it to be eaten at dinner. As head of the family, Pereduras had to cut open the fish and there, in its belly as the knife sliced through it, was his precious ring. Somehow, the fish had swallowed it and there was a great rejoicing at its return to the family, but never again did Pereduras wear that ring while out in the countryside.

Its discovery has given rise to the name of the market town which was home to Pereduras and his family. It was called 'Pike-a-Ring', and a pike features in the town's coat of arms. Today, the nickname for the local football team is The Pikes.

During the last century, some wooden piles and other traces of lake dwellings were found in the still waters. Could they be the remains of Pereduras' palace? If so, where is the ring now?

The pond can still be seen beside the A170 as it enters Pickering from Kirbymoorside. Westgate Carr Lane leads past it. That huge spring-cum-pond produces a stream which flows along the western edge of the town, heading south-west into open fields. It joins the River Rye some five miles south of Pickering.

There is another story of Pickering which deserves inclusion. Years ago, there was a very unholy monk who was a resident of Rievaulx Abbey near Helmsley. He fell to every temptation, enjoying the companionship of loose women, too much wine and food, and all the temptations that one of his calling should resist. The Devil heard about this monk and recognized a potential recruit.

One night, therefore, Satan paid him a visit and promised as many beautiful women as the monk wished, along with all the food and drink he could cope with, plus any other luxury or delight that he may desire. The monk listened to this offer and asked if there was any condition.

'Yes,' said the Devil. 'If I provide you with all these

things, you must sign a promise to me. You must agree that, in twenty years time, you will give me your soul.'

The monk considered this offer and said, 'I will agree if I can also make a condition.'

'And what is that?' asked the Devil.

'You can have my soul as promised if, upon my death, you can find one honest man and one virgin in Pickering.'

'Done,' agreed the Devil.

But when the monk died, the Devil could not find either of those people in Pickering and for months afterwards, vent his anger by arranging thunderstorms and lightning around Rievaulx Abbey. The cunning monk had defeated the Devil.

19 Robin Hood's Bay

A haven for an outlaw

In spite of the name of this fascinating fishing village and the names of some nearby land features, there is no firm evidence to link Robin Hood with the bay that bears his name. There are discrepancies about the period of the Robin Hood legends themselves, some authorities believing them to date to the eleventh century, others claiming the legend started at the time of Richard I (The Lionheart) in the twelfth century and others asserting that Robin Hood was made an outlaw at York Assizes in 1225. Certainly, a Robin Hode failed to appear at those assizes in 1225 and was therefore declared an outlaw; there is also written reference to Robin Hode in 1261 in Berkshire where he was depicted as a scoundrel. In 1317, a Robert Hode of Wakefield disappeared after failing to report for military service and this Hode had a wife called Matilda, then the traditional name for those called Marian. Two years earlier, this couple paid two shillings for a piece of land at Bickhill near Wakefield and there built a five-bedroomed house. This Robert Hode once fought for the Earl of Lancaster against Edward II at the Battle of Boroughbridge; the Earl lost and Robert, as a rebel, was outlawed.

In 1324, another Robyn Hode was paid for service to Edward II as a valet. There is also a suggestion that Robin Hood was really Robert Fitzooth, the heir to the earldom of Huntingdon and, whichever was the true outlaw, he is irrevocably linked to Nottingham and Sherwood Forest, the latter now being a tourist attraction due to his exploits.

Robin Hood, however, had a string of Yorkshire connections, the most famous of which surrounds his death at Kirklees Priory. The prioress, a relation of his, bled him to death at the age of almost ninety. She was called Elizabeth Stainton, and at that time thought Robin had earlier killed her brother. Pretending kindness, and 'being skilled in chirurgery', she cut an artery in his arm and bound it so loosely that the famous outlaw bled to death. In his final moment, he realized what was happening and shot an arrow from the priory, asking to be buried where it fell. His grave is now in the grounds of Kirklees Park where a roughly hewn stone bore this inscription:

Here underneath this little stone
Lies Robert Earl of Huntingdon.
Ne'er archer was as him so good
And people called him Robin Hood.
Such outlaws as he and his men,
Will England never see again.
Died November 24, 1247.

Elizabeth's grave is nearby, Elizabeth being the first Lady Superior of this Cistercian convent which was dedicated to the Blessed Virgin Mary and St James. Her tomb stone asked that Sweet Jesus of Nazareth, Son of God, take mercy on her.

One very strong theory is that Robin Hood lived and operated in Barnsdale which is near Wakefield and that his exploits actually took place in the Went Valley near Pontefract. He is said to have purchased a plot of land which was in fact the market-place of Wakefield in 1316. He married Maid Marian at Campsall church between Wakefield and Doncaster.

Lord Miles (Bernard Miles) once said Robin Hood was actually born in the North York Moors at the hamlet of Hartoft near Rosedale Abbey and, having married Marian, came to live at Hartoft where he was once accused of poaching. He bases this on the fact that there was a Robin of Hartoft and in support, there is a Robin Hood's Howl at nearby Kirkbymoorside. But there is no evidence to support this idea.

Much of the basis for the Robin Hood legend arises from a collection of thirty-eight ballads, some of which originated in the Middle Ages. The best was known as *A Geste of Robyn Hode*, a collection made around 1500. It seems that, throughout history, there have been many Robin Hoods, most of them emulating the deeds of the original bowman and outlaw whoever he was, and wherever he operated. In North Yorkshire, however, there is an entire village named in his honour.

Robin Hood's Bay sits literally on the edge of the sea between Whitby and Scarborough, the older cottages crowding the shoreline. So close are they that there is one story of an inn's window being smashed by the bowsprit of a ship, and at high tide, the sea literally flows up the main street. In 1892, John Leyland said it was 'one of the quaintest places imaginable; it hangs in picturesque confusion on the steep sides of a narrow gulley; it is yet another of those North Yorkshire fishing villages which clings to the cliff and whose houses continue to drop into the sea.' Indeed they do. From time to time, a cottage or bungalow on the cliff top has vanished into the waves, although the older houses cling to the cliff in a most remarkable way. Narrow passages and steep steps divide the cottages and Arthur Mee said that it was one of the most astonishing sights on the Yorkshire coast.

Robin Hood's Bay was a smugglers' delight and there are wonderful echoes of fishing lore here. It is a mecca for artists and writers, and features as Bramblewick in Leo Walmsley's book *Three Rivers*, later filmed as *The Turn of the Tide*. He lived here from 1894 until 1913. There is a car-park at the top of the hill and a breathless climb from the sea-front for those who wish to savour the delights of the shoreline. The tide does come in very rapidly, and it can be dangerous to spend too much time on the beach.

Having explored this lovely village, the visitor will

inevitably ask: 'Did Robin Hood ever stay here?' Surprisingly, the village makes no claim that the outlaw ever called or lived here and I know of no formal 'Robin Hood's trail' or anything similar. The name of the village is sufficient to excite interest. Oddly enough, it was not called Robin Hood's Bay until the time of Henry VIII, around 1532, which was some three centuries after the hero's death. It was then called 'Robbyn Huddes Bay', although some believe this referred to the bay itself rather than the village. Around the bay are other communities like Raw and Fylingthorpe, and the main village was once known as 'Bay Town' or even 'Robin Hood's Town'. Today, the name Robin Hood's Bay applies to both the village and the bay. But did the outlaw ever visit Robin Hood's Bay?

To the south of the village, overlooking the sea, is a hill called Stoupe Brow upon which are Robin Hood's Butts. These are shown as such on modern maps, and although we might regard them as ancient earthworks or burial mounds, legend says this is where Robin Hood and his Merry Men practised their archery. The lofty elevation afforded fine views over the countryside and seashore which meant they could maintain a careful watch for approaching enemies while undergoing their essential training. One story says that Robin fired an arrow from Stoupe Brow and it landed in the bay to pinpoint the site of the village which bears his name.

The question remains, however, that if Robin Hood, and his band of Merry Men in Lincoln Green operated in either Sherwood Forest or in Barnsdale, why would they practise archery many miles away on the Yorkshire coast?

The answer was that Robin was frequently harassed and pursued by soldiers and by the men of the Sheriff of Nottingham, all of whom wished to put an end to his career. To escape them, he needed a sanctuary – and he found it in the place now called Robin Hood's Bay. According to the historian Lionel Charlton in his *The History of Whitby and of Whitby Abbey* published in 1779:

In the days of Abbot Richard and Peter his successor

[abbots of Whitby Abbey in the twelfth century], lived that famous and renowned outlaw, Robin Hood who took from the rich that he might have wherewithal to give to the poor. He many years kept under him a considerable number of men who lived by rapine and plunder.

He resided generally in Nottinghamshire or the southern parts of Yorkshire; but when his robberies became so numerous, and the outcries against him so loud, as almost to alarm the whole nation, parties of soldiers were sent down from London to apprehend him. And then it was, that, fearing for his safety, he found it necessary to desert his usual haunts and, retreating northward, to cross the moors that surrounded Whitby where, gaining the sea-coast, he always had in readiness near at hand, some small fishing vessels to which he could have refuge if he found himself pursued.

For in these, putting off to sea, he looked upon himself as quite secure and held the whole power of the English nation at defiance. The chief place of his resort at these times, to which he communicated his name and which is still called Robin Hood's Bay, where his boats were generally laid up, is about six miles from Whitby. There he frequently went a-fishing in the summer season, even when no enemy approached to annoy him and not far from that place he had butts or marks set up where he used to exercise his men in shooting the long-bow.

Charlton went on to say that until 1771, it was believed these butts had been especially constructed by Robin Hood for archery practise but in that year some human bones were found and it was realized they were the burial places for the dead, probably being used as such by our pagan ancestors. This, however, did nothing to spoil the myth.

The notion that Robin Hood came regularly to Robin Hood's Bay to escape capture or merely for a break in his hectic life, is one which continues to this day. It is claimed that he used the name of Simon Wise during these visits, this being to deceive any pursuers for the local people knew his true identity and they protected him. While among them, he was a good, kind man who attended Mass every day and who had a special devotion to the

Blessed Virgin Mary, while being described as an arch-robber 'but the gentlest there ever was'.

He was known to have a background of quality, being entitled to a coat of arms – this was 'Gules, two bends, engrailed Or' – and he would even rob from bishops and churches to aid the poor.

While at Robin Hood's Bay, he spent many happy hours fishing and would put to sea the moment his spies warned him of the approach of any suspect soldier or official and he would remain at sea until the danger had passed. There is one story which says that, as a first-time fisherman, he did not know it was necessary to bait the hooks, for he simply cast his line into the water with a bare hook.

It is said that he loved to visit the beach and even went as far as Scarborough and Whitby, sometimes joining the crew of a local fishing boat and he once helped to defend a Scarborough boat against a French man o' war.

With a theory that many good legends have some basis in fact, it does seem probable that Robin Hood did visit the bay which bears his name. It is also likely that he was accompanied by his band of outlaws and by Maid Marian so perhaps they were among the first tourists to arrange organized trips to this fine coastline?

For another tale of Robin Hood see the chapter on Hawsker.

20   Roseberry Topping

The death of a baby prince

Roseberry Topping is one of the most visible of the landmarks of the North York Moors. It stands a short distance from the north-western edge of the moors and is a conical-shaped hill which is just over 1,000 feet high. Half-a-mile or so within the boundaries of the national park, it is almost midway between Great Ayton and Guisborough, just off the A173, and is likewise a short distance from Middlesbrough. Several footpaths climb to the summit from where there are magnificent views in all directions.

Its distinctive outline has led to it being likened to a miniature Fujiyama, a miniature Mont Blanc or even a mini Matterhorn. Certainly, the local people regarded it as a mountain, many erroneously claiming it was the highest peak in Yorkshire. At 1,051 feet high, it is not especially lofty; some parts of the nearby moors are higher than Roseberry, but its location and its shape have given it a fame all of its own. If some reference books claim that Roseberry is higher than 1,051 feet then this was once true. The quarrying of stone, followed by subsidence at the summit, have reduced its height over the years but the legendary height of Roseberry is featured in a lovely dialect yarn called *The Register Office* by John Reed.

Speaking of Roseberry Topping, one of his characters called Margery Moorpout says, 'Ah thowt onny feeal hed knawn Roseberry. It's t'highest hill i' all Yorkshire. It's aboot a mahl an' a hawf heagh an' as cawd as ice at t'top i' t'yattest day i' summer.'

Roseberry's distinctive features are the result of millions of years of erosion around it, but the hill's cap of tough sandstone has protected it. For this reason, in geological terms, it is called an 'erosional outlier'. Close to the top, a layer of oolitic clay has made it a classic site for fossils, while in 1826, a quarryman working on the western side of the hill found several prehistoric tools in a crevice, including axe heads and knives.

Bought by the National Trust in 1985, Roseberry Topping now stands in two counties. The boundary between North Yorkshire and Cleveland runs directly across the summit while the village at the foot, known either as Newton-in-Cleveland or Newton-under-Roseberry is in Cleveland, having been part of the North Riding of Yorkshire until 1974. Newton's parish church is dedicated to St Oswald and has some Norman remains, one carving depicting a dragon attacking a four-legged animal, perhaps a wolf or a dog; but I know of no dragon legend linked with Roseberry.

The name invariably excites interest. The word 'topping' is used to describe other moorland hills of this conical shape, for example Blakey Topping, and it comes either from the Old English word 'top' for hill or the Danish 'toppen' meaning peak or summit.

The prefix 'Roseberry' however, provides scope for more discussion. In the twelfth century, it was called 'Othenesburg', 'Ohtneberg' or 'Othenburg', later becoming 'Ouesbergh' and then 'Ounsbery' by 1610. There is a possibility that, in Viking times, the hill was sacred to the god Odin who was the Scandinavian equal of Woden, although there I know of no record of the hill being known as 'Wodenesbeorg' or 'Wodensburg'. In local folk stories, however, it was widely referred to as Odinsberg. It seems that the transition from Ounesbery to Roseberry is a result of changes in local pronunciation, with the village of Newton once being known as 'Newetunie sub Ohtnebercg'. One theory is that

Roseberry might derive from an old English word, now obsolete: 'rosland' meaning heathery or moor land which had a Welsh equivalent of 'rhos'. Whether Rosedale comes from this source, or from the Old Norse 'Russi's Dale' is open to conjecture, but the local pronunciation of Rosedale is still 'Rossdle'.

On the southern slope of Roseberry Topping is Airyholme Farm where the father of the famous explorer and navigator, Captain James Cook, found work. Captain Cook was educated in nearby Great Ayton and himself worked on the farm for two years. The family graves are at Great Ayton. Also on the upper slopes close to the summit there used to be a well or spring known as Roseberry Well whose waters were said to be useful in curing ailments such as rheumatism and eye disorders. All that remains is some boggy ground high on the hill.

On the top of the hill, there used to be a hermitage called Wilfred's Needle. This was hewn out of solid rock, but quarrying work and mining for iron-ore around the summit have led to its disappearance, along with the crumbling of some of the topmost layers of land, causing Roseberry Topping's height to be reduced over the years.

There is a long-surviving piece of weather lore associated with Roseberry Topping which goes:

> When Roseberry Topping wears a cap
> Let Cleveland then beware of a clap.

This dates to the seventeenth century, and suggests that when there is mist or cloud over Rosedale's summit, then the surrounding countryside can expect stormy weather.

Roseberry's most enduring legend concerns the sad fate of a young Northumbrian prince and it is often erroneously quoted as the origin of the name of nearby Osmotherley. (The real source is probably 'Osmund's Leah' – Osmund's clearing, via 'Asmunderlac', 'Osmundeslay', 'Osmondirlay' to 'Osmotherley', but who wants to spoil a good story?)

Long, long ago, there was a king of Northumbria called Osmund. His kingdom included that part of England which was north of the Humber and south of the Scottish borders. The district of the North Riding of Yorkshire called Cleveland was then part of his kingdom. In spite of ruling such a fine piece of country and living in such magnificent castles in wonderful surrounds, Osmund was unhappy.

His greatest sadness was that he had been unable to produce a son and heir to this great kingdom. In spite of being happily married for many years, his Queen had not produced a child. He prayed hard and even consulted wise men and magicians, and then, to his delight, he learned that his Queen was to have a child. He ensured that she obtained the very best of attention and consequently, one fine summer day, she gave birth to a baby prince called Oswy.

Osmund wanted Oswy to have the best of everything, and so he consulted more wise men in the hope they might foretell something of the boy's future and his requirements. But the wise men did not have good news.

'Sire,' they said as they sought audience with their King. 'We have only sad news about your son, news of a great harm.'

'Then tell me, that I might work to protect the child from whatever might injure him,' demanded the King.

They told Osmund that his baby prince would thrive until he was two years old, but on the day he reached two years of age, the baby would be drowned. That was their prediction. The King and Queen would be left childless, and there would be no heir to the kingdom. Osmund did not argue with the wise men, realizing that their methods of foretelling the future were the best in the country. Instead, he made plans to thwart the outcome of their prediction. He knew that, on Oswy's second birthday, he must ensure that the child was kept well away from any rivers, ponds and streams.

Furthermore, no one who might harm him or be careless in the way they looked after him, must be left in charge of the infant. Only the Queen, the boy's devoted mother, was capable of the necessary care. As the boy's second birthday approached, therefore, Osmund outlined his plans to the Queen.

'You must take the child to the highest part of the land,' he told her. 'Take him to the summit of Odinsberg and make use of the old hermitage for shelter. Take enough food and clothing for three days and there you will be secure from dangerous waters. On the summit of Odinsberg, there will be no risk of drowning.' The Queen obeyed.

Taking the child by the hand, they began the long climb to the summit of Odinsberg. It was a hot, dry day and the little boy was restless and weary, so his mother had to carry him for much of the way, especially over the final climb. It was exhausting work, for she had to carry their food and clothing too, but, by evening, she had found the old hermitage on the summit. It was a dry, cool cave with a bed of bracken and enough sticks to light a fire if the night became too cold. Due to their exertions, they slept well that first night, although the Queen had bad dreams about the following day for that was the second birthday of Prince Oswy.

On the day of Oswy's birthday, therefore, she awoke early and made her preparations. She had brought some goodies and some toys and presents with which to while away the long hours.

It was a hot and sunny day, ideal for sitting in the open air to enjoy the warmth and light. As the sun climbed into the sky, the day became hotter and hotter, but the tiny prince seemed not to notice. He played with his new toys at the entrance to the hermitage as his mother relaxed. The heat was almost unbearable and so she went into the cave for a few moments of coolness; lying down on the bed of cosy bracken, she fell asleep.

The baby prince was still outside, playing on the flat earth near the entrance, but as she slumbered in the heat of the day, the child wandered off. With no mother to protect him, he began to explore the summit of Odinsberg.

Something must have warned the Queen for she awoke with a start and immediately realized the boy was missing.

She rushed outside, crying his name and searching the area outside the cave, but there was no sign of Oswy. She searched for many minutes and then found him. His tiny body was lying face down in a pool of water close to the summit; these were the waters of the Odinsberg Spring, the curious spring that produced a flow of water from the top of the mountain. She clutched the cold and still form to her bosom and did her best to revive him, but it was too late. The tiny Prince Oswy was dead, drowned as the wise men had foreseen.

Oswy was buried in a church at Tivotdale but his mother was so overcome with remorse, blaming herself for his death, that she died soon afterwards.

King Osmund buried his Queen at the side of his son, and later entered a monastery in an attempt to overcome his own grief.

From that time, Tivotdale was given a new name. It was called 'Oswy-by-his-mother-lay', and is now known as 'Osmotherley'.

21 Runswick Bay

The Hob Hole Hob

For detailed information about hobs, turn to chapter eight which features Glaisdale and the famous Hart Hall Hob. As that chapter explains, hobs frequented several inland regions of the North York Moors, but in the case of Runswick Bay, there was a coastal hob.

Runswick is yet another of those delightful red-roofed fishing villages of North Yorkshire whose cottages cling to the cliffs in a most intriguing manner. Lying only a mile or so from the A174 Whitby-to-Guisborough coast road, the village can easily be overlooked but it is certainly worthy of the small diversion. There is a spacious car-park near the foot of the steep hill where shops, cafés and holiday cottages abound within yards of the sandy beach.

The village reclines in a sheltered bay, but visitors must beware of the rising tide which can rapidly cover the beach to trap the unwary. Nonetheless, the bay is popular with pleasure craft and there is usually a line of fishing cobles near the shoreline, a reminder that Runswick is a fishing village like nearby Staithes. The lifeboat, always standing-by, is a constant reminder of the risks taken by the fishermen and there is a heartwarming story of 1901 when the women launched the lifeboat to save their husbands who were all caught in a storm.

Overlooking the Bay on the eastern side is the jutting bulk of Kettleness Point which stands almost 400 feet high; long ago, it supported a Roman signalling station and today there is a coastguard station, a ruined chapel and a few isolated cottages. A century and more ago, these cliffs were mined for iron-ore and the excavations at their bases caused the cliffs to collapse. On 17 December 1829, a mass of the cliff at Kettleness fell into the sea, taking the entire hamlet with it (see chapter fifteen).

Runswick has also suffered from sea storms. One of them washed away a complete iron works comprising two furnaces, an engine house and a chimney: if the sea did not claim the cottages, then the sliding cliffs did. There are several accounts of the undermined cliffs sliding into the sea, taking houses with them. In a landslide in 1682, the whole village, with the exception of just one cottage, perished in a storm as the homes slid down the cliff but, oddly, no lives were lost. New coastal defences have helped to alleviate this kind of problem, but landslides are still a regular occurrence.

In common with many of fishing villages, Runswick used to be riddled with superstition and folklore. There are accounts of fishing boats being burned after a sea tragedy and of cats being sacrificed as the boats returned from fishing, this being to ensure a safe landing. As the boats came in, the children would dance around cliff-top fires singing to ward off any impending bad weather. The main song was:

> Souther, wind, souther,
> Blow father home to mother.

When the children of Runswick Bay used to suffer from whooping cough, known locally as the kink cough, there were some strange cures. One was to take a suffering child onto the moors behind the village and cut a hole in the turf. The child's mouth was held close to the newly revealed earth and they were told to inhale, the belief being that fumes from the soil would cure the cough. This idea persisted well into the early years of this century; but there was another, more romantic, method of curing the kink cough which involved a visit to the cave where the hob lived. It was known as Hob Hole and it is still shown on the maps in the centre of the shoreline of Runswick Bay. In fact, the original cave was destroyed several years ago by jet diggers but the legend persists.

The Hob Hole Hob lived in that cave, so the people of Runswick Bay believed, but we have no specific description of him. He was probably similar to the other hobs, a small, elf-like man with no clothes, for his body would be covered in thick brown hair. Like most of the moorland hobs, he would be mischievous, but he could do good when the occasion demanded. In this case, his speciality was the curing of whooping cough in children and the mothers sincerely believed he was capable of this.

When a child was suffering from whooping cough, the mother would carry the patient down to the beach and walk along to the mouth of the Hob Hole. There she would halt as she called out:

Hob Hole Hob,
My bairn's gotten t'kink cough,
Tak it off, tak it off.

There is no recorded payment or gift for this service, and there are no notes about whether any successes were achieved, although there are some accounts to suggest that there was an improvement. Any improvement was probably a kind of faith healing or even due merely to the course of nature.

This odd belief, however, lingered until around 1900, and the hob is honoured by having his 'surgery' mentioned on modern Ordnance Survey maps of the North York Moors. (Note: there could be a link between this hob and the bogles of Claymore Well mentioned in chapter fifteen. That well lies but a few yards from Hob Holes).

22 Sexhow

The Worm of Sexhow

A guidebook published around the turn of this century says that, 'Sexhow is a roadside station on the line from Stockton to Whitby.' That guidebook contained nothing further about this small, widespread community and today, it does not even have a railway line. The tracks, now dismantled, ran about a mile to the south of Sexhow, for this was the route from Stockton-on-Tees to Whitby via Stokesley and Battersby Junction. Sexhow was one of the stations along this route but the old buildings have been altered until they are almost unrecognizable as ex-railway premises.

Details of Sexhow's early history are scarce; it did not warrant a mention in the Domesday Book although the lands here were acquired by a noble family through Peter de Brus, an ancestor of the famous King Robert the Bruce. Upon Peter's death, the estate passed to Marmaduke de Thweng, thence to the Gower family and eventually, in the time of Richard II, to the Laytons whose descendants lived here for many later generations. They occupied a manor house on the banks of the River Leven.

The hamlet's name has been variously spelt as 'Sexou' (twelfth century), 'Sexhowe' (thirteenth to fourteenth), 'Saxhow' and 'Saxo' (fifteenth century), while 'Sexhow' is the modern spelling.

The name comes from 'Sek's Mound', Sek probably being a Norse settler. By the eighteenth century it was called 'Sexhow' or even 'Saxhoe'. It then comprised only six farmhouses and forty-four inhabitants. Today, there is a scattering of farms and cottages; there is not even a church or a pub and no village as such. Sexhow Hall stands beside the road about a mile from the old station and overlooks the River Leven; it is now a working farm. Geographically, Sexhow lies half a mile or so to the south-east of Hutton Rudby and is slightly more than a mile to the north of the North York Moors National Park boundary at Swainby.

In spite of its tiny size, Sexhow does feature in the folklore of the North York Moors for it boasts two enduring tales.

One concerns a greedy farmer who lived here. One dark night, he was visited by the spirit of Awd Nan; in life, she had been a local witch and was now haunting the area in which she had previously lived. When she appeared to the farmer, however, she told him about a chest of gold and silver which was hidden in Sexhow and added that if he consented to an agreement with her, she would reveal the hiding place to him and only to him. He agreed. She explained that the condition was that he could keep all the silver, but all the gold in the chest had to be handed over to her niece who had always lived in poverty. The farmer agreed to these terms and was told that the chest lay beneath the roots of an apple tree in his own orchard.

Awd Nan explained which tree grew above the chest and so the farmer immediately began to dig. He consequently found the chest as Nan had indicated. It was full of gold and silver coins, more than enough to make him a rich man. The sight of such wealth, sadly, was overpowering and all thoughts of honesty vanished from his mind. He reasoned that as he had taken the trouble to dig for the chest, plus the fact that it had meant uprooting one of his precious apple trees and furthermore that the money was hidden on his own land, he was entitled to keep the lot. After all, the message had come to him from a ghost ... maybe it had only been a dream? He therefore decided not to give any of the contents to Awd Nan's poor niece.

From that moment, everything began to go wrong with

his farm and his life: he took to drink although he had always been a teetotaller, his crops failed, his animals became sick and then his own health began to deteriorate. His illness was aggravated by his drinking and very soon his entire lifestyle had regressed to one of poverty and depression.

One Saturday night, after a long drinking session in Stokesley, he was riding home when he felt someone else upon his horse. The other person's spurs dug into the horse's ribs and soon it was galloping almost out of control as he fought with the terrified, racing animal. Neighbours saw him dashing past their homes shouting 'I will, I will, I will' and some accounts said that a little woman in black with a huge hat was sitting astride his horse, urging it on and shouting at him.

She clung to his back in the manner of a cat and he could not shake her off. She screamed and ranted at him as he made his horse gallop violently along the lanes, hoping to rid himself of this old woman, but it was impossible. Finally, in desperation, he made his horse jump over the high gate into his own farmyard, hoping this would dislodge the old woman, but it did not. It succeeded only in throwing him off. He took a terrible fall at that gate and was found next morning by his neighbours. He was lying dead beside the gate for the horse had found its way into the stable. The Ghost of Awd Nan has never since been seen.

The second story about Sexhow concerns an act of bravery by an unknown knight. Not far from Sexhow is a small rounded hill or knoll and the story is that a pestilent dragon lived there. One likely hill is Whorl Hill which is very prominent when viewed from Sexhow. It overlooks Whorlton, a tiny place with stunning views across the plain below, and which is rich with surprises; it has a fascinating castle and an equally fascinating church. One little-known feature is that the conifer trees on the slopes of Whorl Hill have been planted in such a way that the Queen's initials, E II R can be picked out in the light and dark shades of their foliage.

The castle was originally surrounded by a moat and the first building is thought to have been built in Norman times by Robert de Meynell. A later castle, whose remains can be seen today, was probably constructed around the fourteenth century. It once belonged to Henry VIII but only a small portion has survived, the fabric being left to the ravages of weather and time. A superb gatehouse bears the coats of arms of the Meynells, the Darcys and the Greys, while the castle has played an important role in Scotland's history. One of the occupants of the castle was the Earl of Lennox whose son, Lord Darnley, married Mary Queen of Scots. It was here that the plans for that marriage were devised.

Nearby, the curious old church stands at the end of a long avenue of ancient yew trees. It is the same age as the castle, being the Norman church of the Holy Cross. It has a roofless nave and ruined aisles, but the tower, built around 1400, is complete with a medieval bell and, in the chancel, still in use as a burial chapel, there is a fifteenth-century east window depicting an angel and a shield in very old glass.

Inside there is a strange stone cross and one of the earliest oaken effigies in England. This is in the form of the figure of a man; it is hollow and he has a dog at his feet in a superb canopied tomb. This probably dates to 1400 or so and is thought to represent Nicholas, the second Lord Meynell who died in 1322.

There is no longer a village at Whorlton. In 1428, a plague reduced the population to only ten and they fled into nearby Swainby.

It is the slopes of Whorl Hill which are said to have once been the lair of a dragon, but another possible location is a mound, now covered in trees, which is beside Rudby church and the River Leven, almost opposite Sexhow Hall. It is easily seen from the footpath which runs from the church along the banks of the River Leven to join the road leading to Sexhow Station. Whichever of the two locations is involved, the dragon wound its mighty coils around the hill as it surveyed the land.

In this region, such dragons were known as worms; they include the famous Lambton worm and the Sockburn worm of County Durham, plus the Nunnington worm which is dealt with in chapter seventeen. The Slingsby serpent and the Handale serpent are also included in chapter twenty-four and twelve. It is my own belief that the Whorl Hill dragon and the Worm of Sexhow form the basis of the same legend; accordingly, I have called it the Worm of Sexhow.

The Worm of Sexhow was a menace to local farmers because it fed exclusively on milk and its demands were huge. It required the milk of nine cows to satisfy its appetite every day. If it failed to get its supply, it breathed its loud, hissing breath across the fields which killed the crops and caused the livestock and poultry to die by the score. So demanding was the worm that the farmers of Sexhow had a terrible time keeping this monster happy and content. It demanded such a lot, consuming milk they could otherwise sell and devastating their farms if they could not keep pace with its huge appetite. When it became angry, as it did very frequently, its behaviour terrified the local people, so much so that many of them left Sexhow. This might explain why it remains such a tiny place!

Sexhow, however, was to benefit from the skills of a champion worm-slayer. One day a knight clad in shining armour chanced to ride through the hamlet. He came upon the monster in one of its most foul moods. Instead of keeping away from it, however, this gallant fellow decided to fight it. Armed with his sharp sword, his shield and his lance, he decided to rid the hamlet of its worm for ever and so a terrible confrontation ensued.

We are not told the details of this battle; we do not know how long it lasted nor do we know the means by which this knight eventually slew the worm, but we do know that he was successful. The dreaded Worm of Sexhow was eventually slaughtered and the villagers were delighted with their new freedom.

The knight rode on; he did not even stay awhile for

refreshments nor did he give his name. He vanished as quickly as he had arrived. To this day, no one knows where he came from or where he went to; we do not know whether he was from overseas or whether he was one of the many brave knights who lived in the North Riding of Yorkshire.

The only thing that remained was the carcase of the slaughtered worm and so the grateful inhabitants skinned it and carried the scaly pelt into their church at Rudby. The village has now expanded and incorporates nearby Hutton, the two now called Hutton Rudby. The worm's skin was suspended inside the church, over the Sexhow pew, and there it remained for many years to remind everyone of the delivery of Sexhow from the awful worm. But when I called at All Saints Church, Rudby, no sign of the Sexhow pew or the pelt remained.

23   Skinningrove

The Skinningrove sea man

Once a North Riding of Yorkshire coastal fishing village, Skinningrove is now part of industrial Cleveland. Situated in a deep valley near Loftus, it can be reached by turning off the Loftus-Brotton road (A174) near the foot of Carlin How Bank. The narrow road crosses and re-crosses the fast-running Kilton Beck as it snakes into this curious seaside community.

Skinningrove is dominated by the bulk of the British Steel works on the cliff above the village (once this was known as Skinningrove Iron Works, a spreading complex which is closely associated with the birth of the iron and steel industry on Teesside). This modernized giant construction continues to employ people from the village, but Skinningrove bears many scars of its industrial heritage.

Remnants of the industry remain along the valley which has many ramshackle sheds and some ugly buildings. Indeed, one guidebook went so far as to say, 'There is little that is beautiful here except the splendid sunsets behind the smoke.' That is perhaps a little too cruel because the landscape around Skinningrove is spectacular and its curved bay is one of the finest along the coast. It has incredibly soft golden sands with a rocky background and towering cliffs along each side. The Cleveland Way footpath passes through the village and provides stunning views from the cliffs with hair-raising stretches threatening to cast the hiker into the waves. These are the highest cliffs in England and boast remarkable views.

The village contains several delightful rows of houses, with Stone Row being particularly interesting, although some other streets appear to have been haphazardly arranged in short bursts of building. There are sheds galore, many serving the local fishing community whose cobles operate from here. They can be seen lined up along the beach, while many of the sheds have piles of lobster pots on their roofs, an indication of the continuing fishing trade which flourishes. Earlier this century, Skinningrove was the home of a prize-winning silver band and there is a small mining museum which is of interest.

Like so many Yorkshire coastal villages, Skinningrove can boast a fascinating legend. It dates to a time long before the iron and steel works appeared on the skyline, and, indeed, long before the alum works that preceded them. Unlike most folklore, this can be precisely dated because a man called Mr Wells recorded the event in 1535. He realized the story was unlikely to be taken seriously, but vouched for its truth by writing, 'Old men that would be loath to have their credyt crackt by a tale of a stale date, report confidently that a sea-man was taken up by the fishers.'

So what was the creature found by the fishermen of Skinningrove? Unfortunately, we do not have a very detailed description, but it is recorded that, after being caught in the nets of the fishermen, the so-called 'sea man' was taken to an old, disused house in the village and kept there for several weeks.

The creature became something of a tourist attraction with people travelling into Skinningrove to have a look at him. Some tried to feed him, but he refused all offers of food, except for raw fish. This he ate in abundance with clear signs of enjoyment and so the villagers had little difficulty in coping with his appetite. After all, catching fish was their chief source of employment.

The account tells us that the sea man was always most patient with his callers, never becoming offensive or truculent, and it seems he was particulary delighted when visited by 'any fayre maides'. If a young woman called upon him, he would sit and gaze steadily at her 'with a very earnest countenance as if his phelgmaticke breaste had been touched by a sparke of love'.

He had no human voice, we are told, but when he tried to communicate with his captors, he 'skreaked' at them. Nothing in the report indicates whether he had arms and legs and we are never informed about his age, size or physical appearance. Nonetheless, there is little doubt that the people were kind to him and that they liked and respected him.

In time, his behaviour became so good that he was regarded as a real member of the community; he fitted in with the events of Skinningrove to such an extent that no longer was he locked in day and night. He was allowed a little freedom. Eventually, however, the inevitable happened: the sea man of Skinningrove escaped. The old account records it in this way:

> One day he prively stole out of doores and ere he coulde be overtaken, recovered the sea whereinto he plunged himself. Yet as one that woulde not unmannerly depart without taking of his leave, from the mydle upwards, he raysed his shoulders often above the waves and makinge signes of acknowledgeing his good entertainment to such as beheld him on the shore, as they interpreted it. After a pretty while, he dived downe and appeared no more.

So what kind of creature was the sea man of Skinningrove? Perhaps it was really a seal of some kind, or could it have been a relation of the Mermaids of Staithes? (see chapter twenty-six).

24　Slingsby

The Slingsby serpent

Many pass Slingsby without realizing that this quiet village contains a great deal of interest. It is just off the B1257 Helmsley-to-Malton road where one arm of the crossroads leads to Castle Howard (famous as the setting for the television adaptation of *Brideshead Revisited*) as another leads into Slingsby's village centre. The main road carries traffic past even though many of Slingsby's houses overlook the highway; however, almost the entire community lies immediately north of the B1257.

There are some interesting houses with lots of open space in the village centre. Some of that space is occupied by Slingsby's noted maypole. There has been a succession of maypoles throughout Slingsby's recent history. Records date to 1799; the tallest, erected in 1895, was ninety-one feet high. One of Slingsby's modern maypoles was damaged both by lightning and the winter gales of 1984, so a new one was donated by Castle Howard Estate. It was erected in a party atmosphere in May, 1985 and bears a lightning conductor. Used for maypole dancing by the children, it gives pleasure to the villagers and boasts nine feet below the earth and forty-one feet above it.

Of further interest is the mystery of Slingsby castle. It stands tall and proud as its dark stones tower eerily above the cottages and hedgerows. Yet, in spite of its prominence, it is rarely visited and is not at all well known. It is not open to the public and its history presents a puzzle to many who see it.

Like something from a Gothic romance, it stands on a windswept site close to All Saints Church and the breeze whispers through the ivy-covered remains. It is not a safe place to visit, for the ruin is dangerous due to loose stones and ill-maintained masonry. Rooks perch on the highest pinnacle while bats flit along the passages at night.

It is surrounded by an empty moat but in spite of its awesome structure, this is not a true castle. It was built as a rather grand house, but was never occupied; it remains a rare example of an Elizabethan-type house, although in fact it dates from the time of Charles II.

Work started in the 1620s on the former site of a fortress built by the Earl of Huntingdon. The builder of Slingsby Castle was Sir Charles Cavendish, a brother of the Duke of Newcastle and a dwarf in stature. He was, however, a brave and clever man, being both a philosopher and mathematician with 'a lovely and beautiful soul'. After ordering the building of this marvellous house, he went to fight at the Battle of Marston Moor in 1644. He had the misfortune to be on the losing side which was commanded by his brother. Both men had to flee overseas to save their lives. Their estates were forfeited to Parliament and consequently the grand house at Slingsby was never completed and it has never been occupied.

With all the appearances of a ruined castle, there are turrets at each corner and a huge vaulted basement with tunnel-like passages branching off. Designed to be two storeys high, there is evidence of huge windows, many smaller rooms and an impressive entrance hall and great chamber. It was to be a very big house for a very little man!

Below the castle is All Saints Church which was rebuilt in 1868. It contains fragments from an older building. Inside there is the time-worn effigy of a knight in chain-mail with a dog at his feet; he bears a sword and a shield and holds a heart. This is thought to commemorate Sir William Wyville who died in the fourteenth century, having achieved fame as the man who slew the terrible Serpent of Slingsby.

Few records remain, but we are fortunate in having some notes made in 1619 which provide details of the battle. The serpent lived in a circular depression in the ground about half a mile from Slingsby; it was more than ten feet in diameter but its depth is not recorded. The serpent, however, was more than a mile long and preyed on human beings who travelled along the lanes. Many perished as they tried to sneak past the serpent's den. The villagers attempted to save lives by diverting the road. Once it ran straight and true in this part of Ryedale, but, with enormous effort, and always in fear of death, they managed to divert the section which led past the serpent's den by creating a wide sweeping curve.

We are assured that the route of that curving road can still be seen if one knows where to look, although the modern road follows the direction of the ancient Roman street in a fairly straight path.

Little is known of Sir William Wyville except that he was a brave knight who could smite dragons as well as any living man; he also had a reputation for rescuing damsels in distress. He was riding his steed along the old road near Slingsby (the one which passed very close to the serpent's den) when he espied the serpent about to devour one of the village maids. She was fair of face, a beautiful damsel named Helena and she had been picking blackberries to make a pie. In her day-dreaming, she chanced to range far too close to the dreaded den. The serpent reached out and encircled her with its body, coiling itself around her until the breath was squashed from her lovely body. She was to be its next meal; a true delicacy, a most tasty dish.

The gallant Sir William, astride his magnificent white charger and with his faithful dog at his side, however, witnessed this horror and never for one moment did he shrink from his duty. As the famous battle cry of the Wyville's rent the air, he spurred his horse forward and had his sword at the ready. Showing the utmost bravery, he plunged his sword time and time again into the wriggling coils of the huge beast and after a super-human effort, he forced it to yield and to release Helena.

She ran to a safe distance, her ribs bruised and her face dark with tears, both of pain and of relief. She watched the mighty battle; the only witness to what followed. As the enormous serpent released her, it turned its evil eyes upon Sir William, espying his horse and his dog. Here were three meals ... but Sir William was not one to flee from danger, nor did he flinch as he continued the long, tiring battle; sometimes he changed hands to relieve the tiredness of his sword-arm but he never ceased in his conflict with the serpent. He attacked it again and again, slashing its hide with his blade, plunging the sword into its tough body, trying to reach its eyes while dodging its ghastly teeth ...

Helena stood and watched until sundown, and saw that the serpent was finally weakening. Its horrible cries filled Ryedale as it realized it was in its death throes; Sir William fought on, stabbing it again and again, now so weak that he could barely lift his heavy sword. He was now on foot, having sent his tired horse back to the manor house while the faithful dog snarled and bit the serpent, doing its best to aid its weakening master. That dog was a large white talbot, a breed of hunting hound which is now extinct.

The serpent eventually fell. Its coils sank weakly to the ground as Helena cheered and wept in her happiness. Sir William smiled at her through the blood, grime and dirt which encrusted his face and in a gesture of victory, he placed one foot on the serpent's head and held his sword high in his triumph.

His brave dog joined him, wagging its tail and rejoicing. Tragically, however, the serpent was not quite dead. In one final throe, it cast them off like specks of dust and bit each of them with its massive poisoned fangs, two quick bites, one for the man and one for the dog. Both fell dead as the serpent also expired.

Helena ran home to tell this story which has come to us down the ages, and that is why the effigy of Sir William Wyville can still be seen in Slingsby parish church with his faithful dog at his feet. And the heart which he holds? Could it represent that of the lovely Helena for whom he gave his life?

25 Spaunton

The treasure of Spaunton Castle

Spaunton is a tiny community on a hill top close to Lastingham and many of its cottages and farms command outstanding views to the north. Access is possible from the A170 (Pickering-to-Kirkbymoorside) road about a mile out of Kirkbymoorside, in which case there is an interesting drive through Appleton-le-Moors. There is an alternative route through Lastingham which, so far as Christianity is concerned, is the region's most historic village. The Norman crypt beneath Lastingham church is unique.

Spaunton is known as the home of the Manor of Spaunton Court Leet and Court Baron which continues to be active. It is one of thirty-one surviving courts leet in England and Wales, many others being abolished or having their jurisdiction curtailed in 1977. A Court Leet is a manorial court of record which deals with petty offences and administrative matters. Spaunton Court Leet controls and manages common rights over Spaunton Moor and in recent years barricaded a farmer's road with barbed wire when he refused to pay a fine of eighty-five pence which the court had imposed. On another occasion the court threatened the North Yorkshire County Council with legal action if it carried out its threat to erect 'No Parking' signs in Hutton-le-Hole and it also fought the local council when it tried to impose a 'no cycling' rule against children on Hutton-le-Hole village green: it won that battle too.

The area around Spaunton was known as Spaunton Forest in medieval times and it belonged to St Mary's Abbey of York; the game within the forest belonged to the King, however, and there was constant friction between the King and the ecclesiastical authorities about the various rights to take game. Another problem was that the adjoining forest, Blansby Park, was owned entirely by the sovereign and there was a frequent crossing of boundaries by hunters, some accidental but many deliberate.

One little-known legend of Spaunton Moors concerns the Hang Man's Stone. Running into the River Dove near Lowna Bridge two miles from Spaunton, is a stream called Swatcha Beck. By travelling along the bed of this beck to the north, one reaches a large stone called Hang Man's Stone. The story is that a thief stole a moorland sheep, killed it and tied its hind legs together. To carry it home, he put his head through the hind legs and allowed the carcase to hang down his back. His neck, aided perhaps by his hands, took the dead weight as he bore home his trophy. The effort of carrying this weight, however, made him tired and he had to rest. He came to the stone in question and sat in front of it, but did not remove the sheep from his back, instead allowing it to lie on the stone; thus was he relieved of its weight. The carcase suddenly shifted, sliding from the stone on the side away from the thief and he was unable to prevent its movement. As it moved, the legs about his neck choked him and he was literally hanged as he struggled to get free. That stone has since been called Hang Man's Stone.

From Hang Man's Stone, a series of standing stones led along the road to Young Ralph and the Margery Stone (see chapter two). In sequence from the Hang Man's Stone, they were: Thorn Stone, Prick in the Thorn, Prick in the Stone or 'Stoup' as it was sometimes called; Saddle Rock or Cattle Stone; Cattle Rook; Rudland Rook; Pike Howe; Cattle Howe; Seven Stones and Margery Bradley. Two other stones on those moors are inscribed Westerdale and Spaunton and are probably parish boundary markers.

In the village itself, however, there is a sad tale of

unfulfilled romance. Many years ago, there used to be a castle at Spaunton. According to legend, it was owned and occupied by the good and brave Robert, the Baron Spaunton. A landowner and benefactor to the community, he had fallen in love with the beautiful Lady Elfleda Kirkby who lived on the south of the moors. They were betrothed and the marriage was to be the following year.

Robert had postponed the wedding because he had a battle to fight. That battle was the first of the Crusades. Pope Urban II had urged all Christians to help recover the Holy Sepulchre and to reclaim the Holy Land from the Moslems. Robert had heard wonderful stories of the work of Peter the Hermit and Walter the Penniless in that campaign, and so he decided that, before he married to produce an heir to Spaunton Castle, he would spend a year fighting with the Crusaders.

Having made his plans and with his white tunic bearing the famous cross symbol, he mounted a superb white charger and sallied forth into battle in a far-off land. Hardly had he galloped out of view, however, when the evil baron Eustace decided to take over the castle. He wanted the castle, its work force, its treasures, its lands and, worse still, he wanted the lovely Lady Elfleda. For months, he had been attempting to woo her in spite of her love for Robert, but she had faithfully resisted all his advances. But with Robert away at the Crusades, there was a chance of success that would never be repeated and the bold, bad baron was not one to miss such an opportunity. He knew that Elfleda would still be at Spaunton Castle, having travelled over the moors to bid farewell to her Robert. The bad baron's raid was well timed and, with a band of dirty, evil men, he marched to the drawbridge which was still down, and within minutes his men were slaughtering all who opposed him.

Robert's men were totally unprepared for this onslaught; many were incapable through drinking too much mead and ale after celebrating the bravery of their knight and so Baron Eustace and his men encountered very little opposition. The only problem was Elfleda. She had locked herself in a strong room at the first indication of trouble, knowing that Robert's men were in no position to defend the castle. Eustace, however, was not deterred and found her easily: he beat down the door and carried her in triumph to the quadrangle where he showed her off to his men.

The air was filled with lusty cheers as Eustace explained his crude plans for the pretty maiden. She had no wish to go along with such debauchery and in a moment when Eustace's attention was diverted, she fled from the men.

'Stop her!' bellowed Eustace as Elfleda ran towards the gate, but the men, clad in heavy armour and weary after their long trek and fighting, were no match for the fleet-footed girl. She managed to reach the drawbridge but it was already being hauled up ... she scrambled to escape, slithering down the rising planks of slippery timber as the heavy chains hauled it higher and higher ... and then she fell.

She fell into the moat which was deep with sluggish and slimy green water and the weight of her dress, heavy with the water, dragged her down. No one could save her; the men, in their heavy armour, were unable to rescue the fair Elfleda and so, tragically, she drowned.

In a mad fit of sorrow and rage, Eustace cried, 'If I cannot have the woman, I do not want the castle. Destroy it. But I will have the land upon which it stands! That shall be my reward. I shall then build my own castle here ...'

Systematically, every stone of Spaunton Castle was knocked down and removed; every piece of evidence was obliterated as Eustace mourned Elfleda. She was buried nearby but his evil plans to acquire the land also failed.

Warned earlier by Elfleda of the likelihood of danger from Eustace, Robert de Spaunton had willed the land to the abbot of St Mary's Abbey in York. The condition was that, should anything untoward happen, the abbot should have custody of the land and everything that stood upon it pending the return of Robert or, in the event of his death, in consideration of the wishes of Lady Elfleda. Even in his absence, Robert had defeated the scheming Eustace and he had also lodged a fortune in gold and silver in a secret chamber below the castle. This was to ensure continuity of the castle, for he did have young cousins to consider as possible heirs. In spite of all his murder and scheming, therefore, Baron Eustace got nothing. He died in misery some years later.

Robert never returned from the Crusaders. No one knows what fate he suffered and, with Elfleda dead, the land which had borne Spaunton Castle therefore passed to the monks of St Mary's Abbey for the abbot to administer on Robert's behalf.

Somewhere in Spaunton, therefore, a fortune lies buried and awaits anyone who can prove he or she is a legitimate descendant of the family of Robert de Spaunton; but first, Robert's will and the deeds must be found. They are awaiting the right person. If the site of that ancient castle can be located, so the legend goes, that fortune and the instructions made by Robert, are buried deep beneath the site of its former chapel.

Many centuries after the demise of the castle, the custodian monks of St Mary's concealed a chest there during the Reformation; this was to keep the deeds and the treasure safe from Henry VIII's plundering commissioners for the monks were still caring for them, even though some 500 years had passed. It is said that the ghost of Lady Elfleda still watches over that treasure, while the ghost of the disgraced and defeated Baron Eustace drags a clanking chain along nearby Hamley Lane.

26 Staithes

The mermaids of Staithes

The A174 sweeps along the coastline between Loftus and Whitby and cuts through the more modern portion of Staithes where semi-detached houses line the main road. The route of this busy road suggests that there is little more to this curious village; but the real Staithes cannot be visited by coach or car, visitors must walk down a very steep hill and must then walk back again having seen this intriguing place. There is a spacious car-park at the top of the hill.

The real Staithes comprises tiny stone cottages which cling miraculously to the sides of the cliffs overlooking the small bay in which the villagers have made their home. It has been described as one of the quaintest places in the kingdom, a place that must on no account be missed and the most remarkable village on the English coast. In his book *Fair North Riding*, the local author Alfred J. Brown, said that only a sea-loving race could have built a village like Staithes because every conceivable obstacle was in the way; but the village was built even if the cottages look in danger of falling into the sea. They have been like that for centuries, with little room for gardens, yards or outside spaces, for Staithes is a true olde-worlde fishing village.

Narrow alleys and steep steps divide the buildings, and the houses huddle together for protection against the North Sea. This has not prevented several being lost – over the years Staithes has sacrificed many cottages; on

146

one occasion in 1745, a row of thirteen was swept away. One of them was the draper/grocer's shop where a lad called James Cook (later the world-famous Captain Cook) had only recently been employed. In 1953, a storm severely damaged the Cod and Lobster Inn which stands on the edge of the harbour: the risk of such damage is always there.

The village does cater for tourists, but happily has no amusement arcades, dodgems or bingo halls. It has retained its essential character and has long been a haven for artists. The women still wear the curious Staithes bonnets, generally white in colour although black ones are worn at funerals. Many of the men still earn their living as fishermen.

The village might well claim to be one of the first to respect equality for women, for as one old guidebook records, 'The men are an honest, stalwart race whose most apparent fault is a prospensity for letting their equally stalwart womenfolk do the major share of whatever work may be going.' Another writer says, 'The men were for the most part watching their womenfolk at work,' and on this occasion five women and only two men are hauling a boat from the sea.

The tough life of fishing has supported Staithes for generations, its people seldom leaving the village to follow other trades or professions.

Even at the turn of this century, it was a very insular community where strangers were not welcomed. The villagers are known as 'Steearsers', the local pronunciation of Staithesers, and one Steearser is said to have been so busy fishing that he refused a request to visit the King of England to tell him about a local boat race between the fishermen of Staithes and those of Blythe in Northumberland.

For all its charm, Staithes does not have an ancient history. There is no parish church for example, although a Roman Catholic one was built in 1885. Records date to 1415 when it was then known simply as 'Staithe'. The word means 'landing place' and it may be that this was merely a landing place for nearby Seaton which has since disappeared to re-emerge as Hinderwell.

For all its lack of ancient history, Staithes has achieved immortality through its association with the world's greatest explorer and navigator, Captain James Cook. He was apprenticed to a grocer called Sanderson and worked in a shop that has since been washed away, although a house in the village bears a commemorative plaque in his memory. It marks his discovery of Australia and other notable voyages; I saw that plaque unveiled by His Royal Highness the Prince of Wales on 31 May 1978 to mark the 250th anniversary of Cook's birth.

Local legend suggests, however, that upon leaving Staithes to become such a noted figure, James Cook had a somewhat inauspicious start.

It is said he stole a shilling (5p) from Mr Sanderson's shop; it is also said that Sanderson discovered the theft and promptly dismissed young Cook. This charge is countered, however, by those who said he behaved correctly by obtaining a discharge from Sanderson, that the money was owed to him and that he did everything in a most correct manner before walking to Whitby to study maritime navigation. Another version is that Cook noticed a South Sea Company's shilling in the till and exchanged it for one of his own, and that sight of the coin triggered his desire to travel. Whatever the truth of the disputed shilling, James Cook did become a great seaman, explorer, navigator and discoverer. Staithes will forever be reminded that he started his career behind the counter of the local grocer's shop.

Like so many of these coastal villages, Staithes does have its own folk story. This one is somewhat different from most because it relates to a visit by two mermaids (see chapter twenty-three for the story of the sea man of Skinningrove). The story begins long before Staithes was a fishing village in its own right, probably when it was merely a landing place for nearby Seaton.

There had been a terrible storm at sea and all the local boats had remained in port, sheltering within the quiet bays. In the rough sea off Staithes, however, two beautiful creatures were being buffeted and bruised by the pounding waves and had become exhausted. They fought against the cruel waves for hours until evening fell and all around was the dense darkness of the northern night. So tired were they that they could not make any headway against the waves and were relieved to see the lights of a tiny village beneath the cliffs. In the dim light, they could distinguish the awesome bulk of Cowbar Nab and below it, a miniature harbour with its collection of fishing cobles. The rocky beach offered sanctuary.

Confident they would survive, they allowed themselves to be swept ashore. Their intention was to remain until the storm subsided, when once again they would be fit enough to take to the water for the journey home.

These were two mermaids, beautiful doe-eyed creatures with the faces and torsos of maidens and the scaly tails of huge fish. With their fair hair sticking to their faces and their arms weary after hours of fighting the waves, they let the tide carry them inland. Both collapsed on the beach at Staithes as the powerful seas crashed and roared in the bay beyond. They fell into a deep sleep, utterly exhausted from their experiences.

Upon awakening next morning, however, they found themselves surrounded by a group of Steearsers who stood and stared and who appeared to be very antagonistic. The mermaids attempted to gain the sea, but the tide had receded and they were a long way from the water. They tried to explain that they meant no harm, and were merely seeking refuge from the storm, but they were seized.

The Steearsers refused to listen to any pleas and hauled the tearful maidens into the village where they were thrown into a lock-up with a handful of raw fish apiece. There they remained while some of the local people threw stones at them, others brought them food and the boys teased them in their nakedness and vulnerability. The mermaids were kept there for four months until the summer, by which time the villagers had grown accustomed to their strange appearance and some even talked with them. They were allowed out of their prison for short periods but always under supervision.

With the passing of the weeks and the charm of the mermaids, the Staithes people forgot that these were creatures of the sea and one morning, as the mermaids played on the beach, they suddenly made a dash for the water. Too late did the villagers realize what was happening and gave chase, throwing sticks and stones to halt the flight of their curious visitors. The pair of mermaids, with a flourish of their tails, had reached the safe water.

The villagers could only stand and watch as the two mermaids swam out into the bay; some youths flung a token stone or piece of driftwood at them, but no harm was done. One of the mermaids expressed her sadness at their treatment during their enforced stay. As she swam away, she shouted her disapproval at the Steearsers, at last being able to vent her anger without any harm resulting.

She halted and rose out of the water, standing on her fluttering tail in a smooth part of the sea as she called a curse upon the village. She said, 'The sea shall flow to Jackdaw's Well.' Then both dived under the waves and were never seen again. The villagers laughed at the curse, for Jackdaw's Well was a long way inland and in no danger from the encroaching waves. It was to the landward side of Seaton Garth and its name came from the numbers of jackdaws which gathered there, dipping their beaks in the cool waters which flowed.

The mermaid's curse, however, did come true and the sea gradually encroached upon the shoreline, taking with it many cherished homes of the Steearsers. As history records, as many as thirteen disappeared in one shocking storm and Jackdaw's Well itself also vanished.

Today, the people of Staithes are more welcoming to strangers no matter what they look like or whence they come.

27 Sutton Bank

The White Mare legends

The summit of Sutton Bank provides one of England's most expansive views. It has been admired by countless visitors through the years, including John Wesley and William Wordsworth and it continues to draw visitors who share in its splendours. It looks west towards the Pennine range across the Vale of York. The view towards the foothills of the distant Yorkshire Dales and even into Durham and Cleveland, takes in many towns and villages; consequently, the viewpoint is a mecca for sightseers and tourists. At the top there is a spacious car-park alongside the North York Moors National Park Information Centre which provides a wealth of information about the area; it also offers refreshments, books and toilet facilities.

Nearby is the Yorkshire Gliding Club whose silent, engineless aircraft soar in the skies while a long-distance footpath, the Cleveland Way, snakes across the top of the bank and around the club's airfield. Visitors are asked not to walk on the airfield but the footpath affords pleasing views of these graceful machines, sometimes during their launches.

The Cleveland Way follows part of an old drovers' road which came this way from Scotland and used a route which still exists near Sutton Bank Top. The long, straight road passes Dialstone Farm which is nearby. This was once a public house and a halt for the drovers, and from here the drovers' road led to the Hambleton Hotel which is on the edge of the A170. Tens of thousands of cattle were driven along this route, something witnessed by William and Dorothy Wordsworth in 1802 when Dorothy wrote of 'little Scotch cattle which panted and tossed fretfully about'. Sometimes, a procession of beasts would be two miles long, each comprising thousands of animals driven by men with dogs. Some stretches of that road have been surfaced and are used by modern traffic, while other sections are now footpaths.

Sutton Bank itself is a long, steep hill about a mile in length. It has three gradients of 1-in-5 (twenty per cent), 1-in-4 (twenty-five per cent) and again 1-in-5 (twenty per cent). It carries the A170 Scarborough-Thirsk road from the heights of the moors into Thirsk which is 5½ miles away, passing through Sutton-under-Whitestonecliff *en route*. In 1984, caravans were banned from this hill because too many drivers were unable to cope, but the view from the summit makes the ascent worthwhile.

It was here, on 6 June 1977, that a massive bonfire was lit to commemorate the Silver Jubilee of Her Majesty Queen Elizabeth II; it was number 82 in a chain of 103 bonfires stretching from Jersey in the Channel Isles to Saxavord in the Shetlands. The first was lit at Windsor Castle.

Other points of interest near the bank top include the site of the famous Black Hambleton racecourse which reached the peak of its popularity between 1715 and 1770.

It became known as the 'Newmarket of the North' and received the patronage of both Queen Anne and George I. The turf is said to be the very best for training racehorses, and strings of them can be seen exercising, for the area is now used as a training ground by nearby racing stables.

Along the bank top, bilberries grow wild and are often used to make delicious pies while a short walk to the south, around the edge of the Gliding Club's airfield, is the White Horse of Kilburn. This huge outline of a horse is carved into the slopes of the escarpment at Roulston Scar above the village of Kilburn. It is 105 yards long by some 76 yards high and is the work of a Kilburn schoolmaster called John Hodgson. He and his pupils carved the horse in 1857 and it is now a landmark for more than seventy miles around.

Rising from the plain below is a small, rounded hill; this is Hood Hill, once the location of human sacrifices, but more recently where the monks of Byland first settled in Yorkshire. In 1138, they came to live here for a while before establishing their abbey, first at Old Byland but later in the valley near Coxwold. The gap between Hood Hill and Roulston Scar is variously known as 'Happy Valley' or the 'Devil's Leap'.

Another point of major interest lies just below Sutton Bank. This is Lake Gormire whose waters glisten like silver in the sunshine as it nestles in a fold in the hills near the foot of the cliffs. It was sometimes called 'White Mere' for this reason.

It is a small lake, something like a third of a mile in circumference and is remarkable because no streams run into it or out of it. It was formed naturally, probably during the Ice Ages, and is rich with wildlife and plants. There is a steep, winding path down to the lake from the top of Sutton Bank and the trek is both stimulating and interesting.

This lake is the source of several legends, some of which feature a white mare. Reminders persist in the name of White Mare Crag, a cliff which overlooks the lake, and White Mare Corner which is on the A170 as it approaches Thirsk. Oddly enough, the white mare stories are in no way associated with the White Horse of Kilburn which is so close at hand. The white mare legends were extant long before the White Horse was carved from the hillside and might arise from a corruption of 'White Mere', this being a local name for the silvery sheen on the surface of the lake, or mere.

Another factor concerns masses of rock which fell from the cliffs in March, 1755, an event witnessed by John Wesley. The fall left a massive white scar which, from a distance, had the shape of a horse. The weathering of the exposed area, plus further falls of rock in the 1890s and more recently, have obliterated that outline. It may have given rise to the name of 'White Mare Crag'.

One ancient story was that Gormire was a bottomless lake, while another tale said that the site once contained an entire village. Apparently an earthquake of enormous severity was followed by the appearance of a cavernous crater which opened up and swallowed the entire community, houses, people and animals too. Then water from the surrounding hills drained into the massive hole and filled it. The legend went on to say that, when the water of Gormire is very clear, the steeple of the church and the roofs and chimneys of the houses can be seen.

Another story says that the Devil created Gormire. He once rode a white horse which stampeded in fear, so much so that he lost control and the horse leapt from the top of the cliff. The Devil was still astride at the time and, as the horse plunged to its death, the Devil clung to it and both crashed upon the ground to make the massive hole which is now Lake Gormire.

Yet another story of the Devil concerns an abbot of Rievaulx Abbey which occupies a nearby valley. The abbot called at a moorland inn late one night and hailed a local knight who was at the inn. He was Sir Harry de Scriven. The abbot said that a man was dying in a distant and lonely cottage on Hambleton Moor and urgently required the last rites of the church. As the abbot's horse was tired, could the knight assist by lending him a horse?

Sir Harry agreed, for he rode Nightwind, the fastest horse in the area. It was a superb black horse and would be most beneficial in reaching the dying man as rapidly as possible. Indeed, Sir Harry said he would ride too, to be on hand …

They set off at a gallop with the abbot on Sir Harry's black horse, and the knight now riding the abbot's tired white animal. Even after its long tiring day, however, the white horse was by far the swifter of the two and it turned towards the huge cliffs above Lake Gormire. Sir Harry could not control it as it galloped headlong towards the cliff … and, with him still astride, it made a prodigious leap from the summit.

As Sir Harry fell to his doom, he looked behind and saw the abbot on the cliff-top, sitting upon his own marvellous black horse. Even as he watched, the abbot changed into the Devil, complete with horns and hoofs, as his cruel laughter echoed around those gaunt cliffs.

There is yet a further story of a white mare. It was a white Arab horse. In its native land, it existed long before the Christian era and was known as 'Kehilan', which means 'Thoroughbred'. It was extensively used by fashionable riders and by the military, for it was the most excellent of horses. This Arab mare belonged to a wealthy nobleman and was in training at Hambleton racing stables near Sutton Bank Top. For some unaccountable reason, she became bad tempered and unmanageable, running away on several occasions. She became unrideable and presented a grave problem both to her owner and her trainer. One of the lads who worked at the stables, a fine horseman from nearby Kilburn, was considered one of the strongest of the riders in the area. He maintained that the white mare could be mastered and he offered to ride her so hard over the three-mile gallop, that she would submit to his control. He said she would not run away with him, nor would he permit her to stray from the course. 'I'll either best her or ride her to the Devil,' he is reported to have said.

He was, therefore, allowed to take out this troublesome mare in an attempt to master her. She permitted him to mount her and then he spurred her into a trot, watched by the anxious owner of the stables and the other lads. He guided the mare towards the three mile gallop, a part of the training ground with which he was very familiar. As he drew further away from the stables on this superb turf, the horse began to gather speed and soon she was galloping headlong across the plain with only the sheer drop of the cliffs ahead. The others raced after the pair but as they reached the end of the gallop, the white mare had vanished and so had her rider. To this day, no one knows what happened to horse and rider. Their bodies have never been found.

Still more drama is associated with the part of the cliff known as Knowlson's Drop. This is close to the bank top and overlooks Hood Grange. In the late 1800s, a man called Knowlson was driving his horse and trap towards Kilburn, having spent a night drinking at the Hambleton Hotel. It was dark and it seems he drove down a steep, grassy slope above Hood Grange and the trap careered out of control.

According to local folklore, he survived the fall, but his horse had to be destroyed. Since that time, the place has been called Knowlson's Drop; the name appears on Ordnance Survey maps published early this century, but not on the 1854 large-scale edition. It seems Knowlson suffered his drop after that time!

Finally, there is an old verse about Sutton Bank which says:

'When Gormire riggs (banks) are covered with hay,
The White Mare of Whitestonecliff shall bear it away.'

28 Upsall

The crock of gold

Upsall is a tiny village on the western slopes of the North York Moors. It is close to the A19 trunk road and is just outside the boundary of the National Park. The village and its approaches enjoy stunning views to the west across the Vale of Mowbray and the Plain of York towards the distant Pennines.

One of the curiosities is Upsall Forge. Built in 1859, it has a large doorway shaped like a horseshoe above which is the date 1859 and the words 'Upsall Town'. With only a handful of cottages and farms, the village has achieved some renown because it has had three castles and is the focus of a famous crock of gold legend.

The first castle was built in the fourteenth century by the Scropes, an ancient and respected Yorkshire land-owning family whose ancestors continue to live in the county. Their associations include Masham, Bolton Castle and many links with both Government and Church throughout English history. Sir Richard le Scrope was a friend of the Black Prince, a member of the King's Council and Lord Chancellor in 1378. His eldest son William was created Earl of Wiltshire by Richard II. Richard Scrope became Archbishop of York but was executed in 1405 for supporting a rebellion against Henry IV.

The family's castle at Upsall, however, fell into ruin. The Turton family built a modern castle in 1872-3, but that was destroyed by fire in 1918, although some remains can be seen near the present building. The new castle was constructed by the Turtons in 1924 and continues to serve as a family home.

On the plain to the south of Upsall Castle is a house called Nevison House. This is the supposed home of William Nevison, the gentlemanly highwayman who was nicknamed Swift Nick by Charles II. It was Nevison who made the oft-told horse ride from London to York on Black Bess; this is now erroneously associated with Dick Turpin.

The enduring story of Upsall concerns a member of the Scrope family and a crock of gold. William le Scrope was undergoing a period of poverty and was having tremendous difficulty maintaining his castle and the jobs of his workforce. One night, as he tossed and turned in his sleep, he had a dream which was repeated for three nights, in which a voice suggested that if he stood on London Bridge, his financial troubles would be over. London was some 250 miles away, an awfully long distance when the only means of transport was by horse or even by foot. William had never been to London but the significance of the dream became so strong that he decided to undertake the journey and risk being proved a fool. We have no details of his long and dangerous journey, but we do know that William arrived safely.

He made his way to London Bridge and was amazed by its imposing structure, a forerunner of the present bridge. People were hurrying backwards and forwards, horses and carts were moving across and the bustle of the city was almost overwhelming for this countryman; with the dream clear in his mind, he stood for hours on London Bridge but no one stopped even to pass the time of day. As the time slowly passed, William came to think he had been incredibly stupid – he must have been, to do this as a result of a dream! He was about to leave when an elderly gentleman stopped for a chat. 'I've crossed the bridge at least three times,' he remarked to William, 'And each time, I have seen you standing here. Are you lost? Or perhaps waiting for someone? Maybe I can help?'

William, not wanting to appear foolish, said, 'I dreamt

about London and this bridge, and so I thought I would come and pay it a visit. I'm just enjoying the experience.'

'That's funny,' said the old gentleman. 'I had a dream too. For three nights, I dreamt of a crock of gold beneath a bottery bush in the grounds of a castle at Upsall. But I have never heard of Upsall and don't know where it is.'

William was astute enough not to say that he had come from that very place, but knew that his dream had come true. After a pleasant chat with the old man, William made his way home with great haste. It took several days, but the moment he returned, he went into the grounds of his castle.

Armed with a pick and shovel, he sought the bottery bush (an old name for the elderberry). He found it without any trouble and began to dig. After digging only a foot into the ground, his spade struck a strong object. He scraped away the soil to find a large earthenware pot which had a curious inscription on the lid and, when he lifted the lid, he saw the pot was full of gold coins.

His dream had been fulfilled, and he took the hoard to his castle knowing that his future was secure. The strange inscription on the lid puzzled him though and he sought help to decipher it. He took it to the inn (which has long since disappeared) and left it with the landlord who placed it on the wall as a curio, for no one could understand it. Neither he nor any of the customers knew it had recently covered a cache of gold. For several years it remained on that wall, puzzling locals and visitors alike until one day a strange, dark man with a large hooked nose, a black beard and a wide-brimmed hat paused at the inn for refreshment. The customers, amongst whom was William, thought he was a Jew. He noticed the curious pot lid and asked, 'Does anyone know where it was found?'

William, ever cautious, said, 'No, it has been here a long time.'

'Do you understand the writing on it?' asked the man.

'No,' said William, and the others shook their heads.

'Then I shall translate it for you,' said the Jew, moving across to study the lines.

After a moment, he said, 'It consists of two lines of poetry – this is what it says, 'Look lower – where this has stood, is another twice as good.'

Only William knew the meaning of that verse and so he rushed home and once more began to dig beneath the elderberry tree. He dug to the level of the first pot and continued much deeper, working well into the evening until his spade struck a chest of wood and metal. On the lid was an inscription exactly the same as that on the pot lid. He opened the chest and, sure enough, found it contained more gold coins, a huge amount which would make him rich and secure.

This time, he did not take the lid of the chest to the inn, but continued to dig yet deeper, working through the night until he came to a third, even larger, chest. This time, there was no inscription on the lid, but it contained yet more riches of gold in coins and plate.

William made sure that the villagers were rewarded for he cared for them, provided them with work and homes, and made them secure during his lifetime and beyond.

Stories similar to this one are told in other parts of the kingdom but in Upsall, some people can still indicate the very place where the crock of gold was discovered.

29 Wade's Causeway

The giant roadmaker of Mulgrave

One of the most enduring of the moorland legends of North Yorkshire is a wonderful mixture of fact and fiction. The facts include Britain's longest and best-preserved stretch of Roman road, a Saxon chieftain called Wade who was of gigantic build, the castles of Pickering and Mulgrave and several hillocks and other features upon the moors. The fiction says a giant called Wade, with his equally huge wife called Bell, built a causeway across the moors so that Bell could travel across the marshy and dangerous wastes to milk her cow; it also claimed that Wade and Bell simultaneously built the castles at Pickering and Mulgrave but as they had but one hammer between them, they tossed it backwards and forwards across the moors, shouting warnings to their playing son before releasing it!

The facts surrounding Wade are interesting. It is known that there was a castle in Mulgrave Woods near Lythe at the Norman Conquest (see chapter sixteen). Some accounts suggest one was here in the ninth century and remains can still be identified, albeit with difficulty. As Nikolaus Pevsner writes, in his classic series *The Buildings of England*, 'What remains of the wall is much overgrown and no-one without a plan would be able to make much sense of it.' It is about three quarters of a mile to the south-west of the existing Mulgrave Castle at Lythe and stands on private property.

John Leland (*c.* 1506-52), the first English antiquary, wrote 'Mongrave Castle standeth on a craggy hille and on eche side of it is a hill, far higher than that whereon the castle standeth. The north hille on top of it hath certain stones commonly cauild Wadde's Grave whom the people there say to have been a gigant, and owner of Mongrave.' 'Mongrave' is an old word for Mulgrave, but this was also known as 'Foss Castle'.

An account of Wade's life says that he was born towards the end of the eighth century and lived until the mid-ninth. He was one of the conspirators by whom Ethelred, the brutal King of Northumbria was murdered in AD 796, an act which greatly angered the King's supporters, although others felt Wade had done a massive service to the people by ridding them of this cruel ruler. To protect himself against the wrath of Ethelred's men, Wade strengthened his castle at Mulgrave. It seems that Wade was heavily involved in the politics of the time, fighting across the north from Lancashire to Northumberland. For over thirty years, the cruel authorities of the latter kingdom, which stretched from the Scottish borders to the River Humber, suffered many attacks by Wade and his followers, as a result of which Wade became something of a folk hero. Known as a man who exerted tremendous power, he was a born leader but was on good terms with the local people, and was considered gentle and tender in all his domestic situations.

Wade was not immortal; he died from what one account says was 'a distemper', while another says he was fatally wounded by Ethelred's next-but-one successor, a man called Ardulph. That fatal wound was delivered at Whalley in Lancashire, four years after Ethelred's death. In spite of his injuries, however, Wade managed to reach Mulgrave Castle, albeit very badly hurt. He died there and was buried near Lythe. Two standing stones marked his grave; they were then twelve feet apart and were said to indicate the immense height of this warring chieftain. The impact he made upon the district has ensured that his name will live for many generations yet to come.

The other major factual part of this legend is now a popular tourist attraction. It is the Roman road on Wheeldale Moor which would have been in existence during Wade's lifetime; it would then have been around 400 years old. It is now under the care of the Department of the Environment and is open to the public at no charge. It runs parallel with Wheeldale Beck 600 feet above sea level and can be reached via Goathland from where it is well sign-posted, and there are other means of access across moorland routes.

The road is sixteen feet wide and around one and a quarter miles long; it is made up of large, flat stones covered by smaller pebbles and gravel, and the centre is raised to permit drainage. There are also drains and culverts. Although it was once smooth, it is now very roughly surfaced, the larger stones protruding to form a very irregular surface. It is a truly remarkable feat of construction, especially when we realize that our own roads were little more than mud tracks until the last century.

This road was part of the Roman network which extended from Malton. One route led towards Hovingham via villages still bearing the suffix 'le Street'. Their names, such as Barton-le-Street, serve as a reminder of their position along a Roman street, as a road was then called. Branching off that street was a road which crossed Ryedale towards Cawthorne where four Roman camps can be seen; from there it stretched over the moors towards the coast, crossing through what is now Cropton Forest and onwards over the moors to Wheeldale. It then followed a route past Julian Park (see chapter nine), and continued past Randymere Reservoir to cross the River Esk near Grosmont. From Grosmont, it crossed the moors to Dunum Sinus which might now be the village of Dunsley. The road probably terminated at what is now Sandsend where there was a Roman cement works, although there was also a Roman signalling station at nearby Goldsborough (see chapter fifteen), each of these possible destinations being close to Mulgrave Castle and the Wade stones.

When the Romans left, this incredible road fell into

disuse and in time was covered with heather and bracken. Those parts which were exposed must have created a great puzzle for our ancestors. There is no doubt that they thought it was a huge highway that had been created by a giant and who better to fit their image than their larger-than-life hero, Wade?

By the Middle Ages, he would have been little more than a myth, but it does not take much imagination to see how the legend grew from the wonderful combination of fact and fiction. The Roman road was not discovered until 1914, and for the next seven years, it was carefully uncovered. To have survived all those centuries on this wet, boggy and bleak moorland makes us appreciate the skill of its builders, but the legend has persisted for almost as long as that incredible causeway.

According to the legend, Wade and his giant wife, Bell, lived in the vast and rugged Mulgrave Castle, having built it with their own hands. They had also built Pickering Castle, some eighteen miles directly across the moors, tossing the hammer between them as the work progressed. In time, they had two fine homes which were separated by miles of inhospitable moorland. Bell, however, had a giant cow upon which the family depended for milk and it was her task to milk the animal. At times, especially in the inclement weather of the exposed moors, it was difficult even for a giant's wife to cope with that daily task, for the moors were riddled with deep and dangerous bogs and the weather could be atrocious. The one thing that would ease the problem was a good road – Bell longed for a footpath along which she could walk in safety to milk her cow and she mentioned this to her husband.

The thoughtful Wade consequently decided to construct a causeway between Lythe and Pickering. In truth, that route bears a remarkable similarity to the Roman road which might still have been intact at the time of the real Wade. The legendary road we know as Wade's Causeway started at Mulgrave, less than a mile from Sandsend where the real Roman road may have met the sea; Wade's

Causeway ended at Pickering Castle, passing within a couple of miles of the Cawthorne Camps on the route of the real Roman road.

Wade's long causeway followed the route of the Romans, but legend says that Bell helped to construct it. She took loads of stones from the beach and from the moors, using her massive apron in which to carry them. Wade used them to construct his road, making a base of the larger ones and finishing with the smaller ones until a smooth surface was produced. A lot of shingle from Sandsend beach was utilized for that final covering. Any surplus or unsuitable stones, especially the very large ones, were cast aside to form small mounds along the route, Bell using her capacious apron for the task. At one stage, Bell's apron strings broke and she lost an entire load of stones, twenty cart loads in fact, and they can now be seen as a higher hill near the causeway.

At various points between Whitby and Pickering, there are many scatterings of isolated stones which fell from her apron during this work. It seems that, from time to time, Wade became angry when things were particularly difficult; on one occasion, he flung a handful of earth at Bell but happily, he missed. The Hole of Horcum is from where he scooped that handful; Blakey Topping is where it landed. They had a son too, and he would watch them at work along the causeway. He copied this act on one occasion when he was left behind on Sleights Moor. He picked up a boulder weighing several tons and threw it at his mother. It struck her but she was not injured; the stone, however, suffered an indentation and bounced off the giantess to land three miles away at Swart Howe. For years afterwards, this stone with its damaged portion, could be seen. Unfortunately, it was broken up for road building some 200 years ago and might well form part of the base of the modern road between Whitby and Pickering.

Near Littlebeck, there is another stone which is a reminder of Bell; it is called Old Wife's Neck due to its similarity to a woman's head, the old wife being Bell.

Wade and Bell did succeed in completing their remarkable highway, and it did ease her daily milking trips, but upon their death the amazing causeway fell into disuse. In time, it was overgrown and many of the stones were removed to build moorland farms and cottages.

Her cow died too, but evidence was found (someone discovered a huge rib) and this was taken to Mulgrave Castle where it could be viewed within living memory even though some doubters said it was nothing more than a whale's jawbone!

Wade lies buried near Mulgrave Castle. Some say his grave is at Goldsborough where there is a standing stone called Wade's stone; others say it is at East Barnby where there is another Wade's stone. The original two stones which were twelve feet apart, have disappeared, and perhaps one of the remaining Wade's stones was, at one time, a marker for his huge grave? The two remaining Wade's stones are a mile apart, but it would be a tremendous giant who was that tall ... but if Wade really did build that causeway, if he really dig a handful of earth out the Hole of Horcum and toss his hammer between Pickering and Mulgrave, then he could have been a mile high! Those two remaining stones might well be the extent of his grave ...

Even today, we local folk do not refer to the remaining portion of ancient road as a Roman road. We always call it Wade's Causeway.

30   Whitby

Submerged bells and fossil snakes

Surrounded on three sides by the moors and on the fourth by the grey North Sea, Whitby is one of Britain's most interesting coastal resorts. It combines an ancient and thrilling history with some spectacular scenery, both in and around it. It has a host of quaint, narrow streets riddled with alleys and yards which meander between red-roofed cottages whilst the picturesque harbour is host to a home fishing fleet as well as to larger boats from overseas, including timber vessels. Fishing has always been a major industry to Whitby and today its kippers are among the finest in the country.

For the visitor, there is a long, sandy beach and a host of fishing and moorland villages to explore, along with the Spa complex and its varied entertainment, Pannett Park with its art gallery and museum and the traditional seaside amusements along the front. Gift and souvenir shops abound, and there is plenty to entertain and amuse both day visitors and those in the town for longer periods. There are some very good restaurants too.

Whitby has an exciting past, being a major whaling port and shipbuilding centre. William Scoresby was a pioneer of whaling and sailed annually for thirty years out of Whitby, capturing more whales than any other person then living. He devised the ship's lookout which is known as the crow's nest.

Between the mid-eighteenth and mid-nineteenth centuries, Whitby was the most prosperous shipbuilding town along this coast, many of its boats being used in Scoresby's whaling expeditions. This heritage, however, goes back much further: Captain James Cook used Whitby-built boats on his expeditions, namely the *Endeavour*, the *Resolution* and the *Adventure*.

It is not surprising that Whitby is a source of literary inspiration too. Britain's first poet, Caedmon, worked at Whitby Abbey while other authors owe much to the town; they range from Bram Stoker who wrote *Dracula* to the novels of Elizabeth Gaskell, Daphne du Maurier, Charles Dickens, Wilkie Collins, Naomi Jacob, Winifred Holtby and local authors Storm Jameson, Dora M. Walker, Mary Linskill and Leo Walmsley who have all made use of Whitby and district in their works. There are many others, far too numerous to list here, and the town has always attracted artists, some of whom remain.

Another boom industry was the manufacture of jet ornaments and jewellery. Whitby jet remains the finest in the land and its popularity soared when Queen Victoria wore jet jewellery. The industry began in 1800; by 1856 it was employing a tenth of the town's population and by 1873 there were two hundred jet shops in Whitby. Imported cheaper, inferior Spanish jet soon began to flood the market, however, and by 1921, the craft had virtually disappeared. Even so, two or three jet workers remain in the town to continue this fascinating craft.

Standing high above all the Whitby glories is one of the nation's most spectacularly sited ruins. This is Whitby Abbey which overlooks the entire town and surrounding countryside from its magnificent cliff-top site. It has recorded some major achievements throughout its long history, one of which was to be the venue of the famous Synod of Whitby in AD 664. This established the system for determining the date of Easter. Another of its achievements was to witness the creation of English poetry through the talent of Caedmon, and in addition it played a significant role in the foundation of the Christian faith in this region. At one stage, Whitby was known as 'Prestebi', the Priests' Town, and the abbey's major achievements came some 500 years before the founding of other famous Yorkshire abbeys such as Fountains and Rievaulx. The time-scale is roughly that which separates the reigns of Queen Elizabeth I and Queen Elizabeth II.

The abbey which stands on the cliff-top is not, therefore, the original. In AD 657, the Abbess Hilda was transferred from Hartlepool to the abbey at 'Streonshalh', as Whitby was then called. Although Hilda is universally known by that name, it seems her correct name was the Anglo-Saxon 'Hild'. (The monks translated this into Latin which produced the name Hilda.) However, the abbey to which she came was a small wooden structure dedicated to St Peter; it was roughly built of tree trunks and thatched with straw, and it remained like this throughout Hilda's reign.

It was replaced by a stone abbey shortly after her death in AD 680 (see Hackness, chapter eleven), but other abbeys occupied the site before the present structure was commenced, probably in 1220. Its end came in the middle of the sixteenth century when Henry VIII established the Church of England. He sent his commissioners to destroy the churches and abbeys of the Catholic faith and Whitby's fine old abbey was ransacked and laid to ruin.

There were further calamities, however. In 1830, on a brilliant day in June, the tall, square central tower of the abbey collapsed without warning; it created a huge pile of stones in the nave which was there within living memory, often covered with flowers and weeds. This collapse removed from the abbey the tower from which Robin Hood and Little John are supposed to have fired their arrows towards Hawsker (see chapter thirteen). Further damage was caused on 16 December 1914 when the German battle cruiser, *Derflinger* (with the Crown Prince on board, so it is said), attempted to shell the coastguard station which stands near the abbey. The shells missed, however, and hit the abbey instead, destroying the gateway and west wall.

The destruction by Henry VIII, however, was by far the worst and has given rise to a legend which still survives.

At the time of its dissolution, Whitby Abbey had a particularly fine set, or 'ring', of bells, described as 'very noble and
antique'. Henry wanted to sell them to raise funds, just as
he had by selling off the gold and silver of such monasteries
and fine abbeys. His instructions were that the bells be
removed from the abbey and despatched by boat to
London where they would be sold. The townspeople were
deeply grieved: if destruction of the abbey was not enough,
then the removal of their bells was considered sacrilegious
and a sense of profound grief settled over Whitby. In
sorrowful silence, they watched as the huge and heavy
bells were slowly transported by horse and cart from the
abbey plain, down the steep lane which adjoins the 199
famous steps, and along to the harbourside where a ship
was waiting. Some prayed for a storm, others prayed that
the bells would never leave the shore, but it was not to be.

In silence they watched as the bells were placed on
board, but there was not a cloud in the sky or a puff of wind
to deter departure of the ship. On a gloriously warm and
sunny day, the ship set sail for London as the townspeople
sorrowed. It is said that many openly wept.

Slowly, the ship slid from its moorings and began the
journey to the harbour mouth, eventually gaining the high
seas beyond the cliffs of Whitby. It was a fine summer
evening and the sea was beautifully calm. There seemed
nothing to prevent the ship reaching London, but when it
reached a point just off Black Nab, a shade more than a
land-mile from the abbey, the ship suddenly sank.

There was no explanation for this – there was no rough
sea, no high wind, no capsizing of the vessel. It simply sank
out of sight and some say it was due entirely to the weight
of the bells. We are not told what happened to the crew, but
the bells are still there. Deep below the waves of the North
Sea, the bells of Whitby Abbey rest on the bottom of the
ocean, and on a very quiet night, so the legend says, it is just
possible to hear them ringing with the movement of the
currents.

There are other folk stories of Whitby, one of which is

internationally known. This is the story of the planting of the Penny Hedge otherwise known as the 'Horngarth Ceremony' or the 'Tale of the Hermit of Eskdale'.

An account is to be found in my own book *Murders and Mysteries from the North York Moors* and in many other folklore collections, so I shall not repeat it here.

One story worthy of inclusion, however, concerns St Hilda, the abbess of Whitby Abbey. She was of noble birth, the daughter of Hereric, a prince of Northumbria. Born as 'Hild' in AD 614, she was baptized by St Paulinus when he was Bishop of York. Her religious education came from St Aidan and at the age of thirty-three, she became a nun. One of her first tasks was to found a monastery in County Durham where Monkwearmouth now stands. Soon afterwards she was sent to another monastery at Hartlepool and was then sent to Whitby, then known as 'Streonshalh', with the responsibility of creating another abbey.

Her intelligence, her faith and her powers of leadership were by this time well established and she was the ideal person for that task and she became known as 'Hilda'. Under her leadership, Whitby Abbey gained a great and international reputation as a seat of learning and of scholarship. Many leaders of the early church received tuition here and the King of France sent his younger noblemen to be taught by the monks so 'that their fragrance might be no longer confined to Yorkshire, but also perfume the palaces of Tours.' St Hilda died on 17 November AD 680 aged sixty-six, being noted as 'that most religious servant of Christ'; she was famous and revered within her lifetime.

One legend said that the birds, especially the sea fowls and wild geese, would never fly over the abbey for fear of soiling it when Hilda was there, and it was claimed that those who flew past the abbey always dipped in flight 'thus to do lowly obeisance to its hallowed precincts'. As the poet Michael Drayton (1563-1631) wrote, 'If this no wonder be, where's there a wonder found?'

Sir Walter Scott mentions this legend as follows:

They told how sea-fowls' pinions fail
As over Whitby's towers they sail,
And sinking down, with fluttering faint,
They do their homage to the saint.

Scott is one of several authors who have recorded a better-known legend associated with St Hilda. In his *Marmion*, he writes of the nuns who told of:

How, of a thousand snakes, each one
Was changed into a coil of stone,
When holy Hilda prayed.

The story of how St Hilda changed snakes into stone lives on in the Whitby area. We know that the 'snakes' were really ammonites, these being an extinct genus of elaborately chambered shell-fish from the family *Cephalopoda*. This was a strange coiled creature because its feet were situated around its head, and it used these to crawl along the sea bed in search of its prey.

The ammonite existed from the most remote of geological times but its numbers vastly increased during the formation of the Lias and Oolite periods. Large numbers existed in many varieties, but they all became extinct during the so-called chalk or Cretaceous period, long before man appeared on earth. Fossilized ammonites have appeared in the rocks around Whitby for centuries; they also turned up in the cliffs and other places, sometimes in stones found high on the moors. These stone 'snakes' gave rise to the legend of St Hilda's worms.

According to the tale, when Hilda was given the task of founding an abbey on the plain above Whitby, the place was so infested with snakes that habitation by humans seemed impossible. There seemed no way of clearing the ground and all attempts failed.

Even Hilda's prayers failed: she prayed that they might all disappear over the cliffs into the sea and never return, but this did not clear the site. However, she was so determined to build her abbey on a pure and clean site, that she obtained a whip. She uttered her prayers for the banishment of the snakes, but this time followed it by cracking her whip at the persistent creatures. On this occasion it worked: the terrified serpents fled before her and most of them threw themselves over the cliffs to crash to their deaths on the beach below.

Many lost their heads in the process, but as each curled up in their death throes, all were immediately turned into stone. Some said the whip had cut off their heads but after that time, no further snakes were found near Whitby Abbey.

It was said that these snakes, perpetually formed in stone, could be found in the cliffs and on the beach for centuries afterwards. That is true – even now, fossilized examples of 'St Hilda's Worms' can be found, and examples of these are shown in the ammonites in the local museum.

The town of Whitby has added strength to the legend by incorporating three of St Hilda's worms in its coat of arms.

The legend of St Hilda was perpetuated in other ways too. Years ago, when Whitby children wished for something very nice, they were told that if, at night when they went to bed, they placed their shoes in the form of a cross and prayed to St Hilda, then their wish would be granted.

Yet another persistent belief, first recorded in 1776, is that during the summer months at around 10 a.m. or 11 a.m., there can be seen a vision of St Hilda in the highest windows of the abbey. To see this, the sun must be in exactly the right place so that its beams fall in the inside of the northern part of the choir. If the sun's position and the time is precisely right, then visitors who stand on the west side of Whitby churchyard, so they can just see the most northerly part of the abbey, past the north of the parish church, can see, in the highest visible window, the resemblance of a woman. She is arrayed in a shroud and is, by tradition, said to be the appearance of St Hilda in her glorified state. Some say the saint so loved Whitby Abbey that she has never left the premises, while others claim it is just a trick of light.

31 Yorkshire Pudding

A plunder blunder

In seeking a stirring yarn with which to conclude this volume, I feel that the story of the plundered Yorkshire puddings is very suitable.

It is one of the proud boasts of the moorland folk that there is always room at the table for the unexpected guest or caller. Down the ages, the people of the moors have been generous with their hospitality, offering refreshment and even accommodation to the needy, and that custom prevails. Should anyone call at a farmhouse or remote cottage around dinner-time (which is mid-day in this part of the world), then they may be invited to join the family at table. At times, there may be no spoken invitation – the lady of the house will simply lay a place setting and will then fill a plate with the meal of the day. That is her invitation for that is the custom of the genuine moorfolk. Refusal would offend.

It is quite possible that one of the delicacies will be a true Yorkshire pudding, an exquisite, mouth-watering dish made as only a genuine Yorkshirewoman is able. It will be large, tasty and hollow, being well and truly risen; it will be light and it will literally melt in the mouth. It will be eaten with gravy, onion gravy being one of the favourites, and, most important, it will be eaten on its own *before* the main course.

The question asked by visitors to Yorkshire is: 'why do you eat Yorkshire puddings before the main course?' The answer lies far back in moorland history and concerns a moorland village whose identity has never been revealed. We know, however, that it was a small community some miles inland and that it comprised three or four farmhouses surrounded by a few thatched cottages and outbuildings. It was typical of the period, the time of the Viking raids, but the villagers, being so remote from the coast, thought themselves secure. Word had not reached this lonely spot that men had landed on the coast in longboats, men with shields and horned helmets, men with fierce tempers and large swords. They were raping and plundering as they burnt down other villages during their attempts to subdue the natives, and not even their victims thought they would find their way into this quiet dale.

Nothing, however, escaped their evil invasion. Their desire to stamp out every relic of the moorfolk and their way of life drove them deep inland. Then, one Sunday at around mid-day, a band of Vikings arrived at this tiny village. They were in a foul mood: they were tired and hungry after days of raping and plundering and they knew that this remote spot would provide them with refreshment and rest.

The band of Vikings, said to be about twenty strong, divided and each entered those lonely cottages, sword at the ready. Some went alone, some went in pairs.

Not knowing of any invasion, the ladies simply regarded them as visitors, for it was dinner-time at each of the houses. Dinner was on the table. When the large, hungry and hairy men burst in, the ladies simply laid a place setting and presented them with a plate full of roast beef, three vegetables and Yorkshire pudding. At this primitive stage of culinary development, the puddings were not eaten separately, they were part of the main course, but the starving Vikings simply sat down and ate the lot. In houses all around that village, the raiders were subdued – it was the Yorkshire puddings that had charmed them. Instead of raping and burning and plundering the village, they asked for more Yorkshire puddings; in fact, they ate the lot and the women had to make more in order to satisfy their enormous appetites.

The village was spared. Instead of suffering harm, it and its occupants escaped the wrath of the Vikings, but the Vikings wished to carry out more raids and so the villagers suggested they cross the hills into a place called Lancashire where the people could be raided with impunity and where it was impossible to obtain true Yorkshire puddings. The raiders left, vowing to return for more Yorkshire puddings when they had completed their work.

The Yorkshire folk, however, did suffer, for the Vikings had eaten all their Yorkshire puddings and their demands had used up all the spare ingredients. There was none left for the villagers that day.

As a consequence, so that they would never again suffer a lack of Yorkshire puddings through generosity to unannounced guests, true Yorkshire folk always eat their Yorkshire puddings before the main course, just in case there is another Viking raid.